THE FUTURE OF
NIGERIA

MICHAEL OWHOKO

ARCHWAY
PUBLISHING

Archway Publishing books may be ordered through booksellers or by contacting:

Archway Publishing
1663 Liberty Drive
Bloomington, IN 47403
www.archwaypublishing.com
1 (888) 242-5904

Because of the dynamic nature of the Internet, any web addresses or
links contained in this book may have changed since publication and
may no longer be valid. The views expressed in this work are solely those
of the author and do not necessarily reflect the views of the publisher,
and the publisher hereby disclaims any responsibility for them.

Any people depicted in stock imagery provided by Getty Images are
models, and such images are being used for illustrative purposes only.
Certain stock imagery © Getty Images.

ISBN: 978-1-4808-9083-1 (sc)
ISBN: 978-1-4808-9084-8 (e)

Library of Congress Control Number: 2020908411

Print information available on the last page.

Archway Publishing rev. date: 5/13/2020

CONTENTS

Preface vii

Introduction ix

Chapter 1   The Historical Development of Nigeria 1
- The Making of Nigeria 1
- Constitutional Development 3
- Fears of the Founding Fathers 6

Chapter 2   The Federal System as an Acceptable Social
Contract 12
- Federal System of Government in the First
Republic 12
- Fiscal Federalism 14
- Principles of Derivation 16

Chapter 3   The Unitary System as the Origin of Nigeria's
Endless Dilemma 19
- Transition from Federal System to Unitary
System by the Military 19
- Abrogation of the Principles of Derivation 22
- Resource Control 23

Chapter 4   The Challenge of Petroleum Resources 26
- Oil as a Source of Revenue for the Government 26
- Oil as Burden on the Niger Delta 28
- Handouts as Alternative to the Derivation
Principle 30

Chapter 5   Solid Minerals Resources Optimism 33
             • Prospects For Revenue Autonomy........................ 33
             • Still A Big Potential 35
             • Developing Solid Minerals Market For Nigeria 36
Chapter 6   The Rise of Agitation 38
             • The National Question, Injustice, and Insincerity. 38
             • Biafra as a Symptom of Discontent 41
             • Militancy as Sign of Frustration in the
               Niger Delta.. 44
Chapter 7   Rescue Efforts 48
             • Failed Attempts at Resolution 48
             • Impact on Nationhood 51
             • A Country on the Precipice.................................. 55
Chapter 8   The Hard Solution 60
             • Options before Nigeria 60
             • Unitarism, Federalism, Confederalism, or
               Break-Up 62
             • Referendum as a Rescue Valve 64
Chapter 9   The Future Outlook 67
             • A blessed nation with potentials.......................... 67
             • Suppressed hopes and missed opportunity 69
             • The outlook ahead 72

Conclusion 81
Endnotes 87

PREFACE

One major temptation faced by authors all over the world is the urge to add new ideas to manuscripts already submitted and scheduled for publishing. However, where the publication process has gone beyond a level that can potentially distort cost structure and optimization, then an option of a reprint and updated edition takes preeminence. This is the status of this book.

Since it was first published with the title: *Nigeria on the Precipice: Issues, Options and Solutions*, new thoughts had resonated, prompting the need for rebrand and inclusion of additional information, necessitating the need for a change of title to *The Future of Nigeria*.

The new title, *The Future of Nigeria*, includes additional key centrifugal forces that are inimical to the unity of the country and the toll they have unleashed on the people, provoking skepticism about the future of Nigeria and causing endless hovering of dark cloud around the country. Literally, what Nigerians see daily is a state of hopelessness while the country is pulled apart by these unhelpful forces.

Besides the centrifugal forces, *The Future of Nigeria* also recognises solid mineral as an important natural resource endowment of the component states that is yet to receive the desired attention from government. If these resources are produced and fully accounted for under a genuine federal system of government, each region or state can self-sufficiently stand on its own without dependency on the centre (the Federal Government) for financial lifeline.

With a strong financial base, each state or geopolitical area will not be petrified joining the growing support clan of those calling for a change of political system and restructuring of Nigeria to a more equitable system that will potentially encourage financial autonomy. The current unitary system masked as federalism where power is concentrated at the centre, breeds nepotism and encourages slothfulness and laziness among the constituent states.

Solid Mineral is therefore highlighted as an important resource that is available in each state or geographical area of the country with the capacity of providing the needed revenue to the regions, which also have the advantage of transforming the mono-commodity nature of the country's economy to a multi-dimensional revenue- based economy.

In addition, the solid mineral is expected to take the spotlight away from the Niger Delta region which plays host to hydrocarbon resources and where there has been youth restiveness resulting from agitation for resource control. Petroleum resources remain the main foreign exchange earner, constituting over 90 per cent of Nigeria's export earnings.

The future of Nigeria becomes a compelling title when viewed against the backdrop of the sociological complex nature of Nigeria and the struggle for control of power and resources by its leaders for ethnic and sectional gains at the expense of national interest, which have consequently led to erosion of premium placed on its future.

Unfortunately, nothing to assure citizens that equity and fairness could be restored to revive declining trust and interest for the unity of the country. However, with proper exploration of the solid mineral across the states of the federation as strategy for economic balance, coupled with a restructured federation, the future of Nigeria may be bright, otherwise, bottlenecks like ethnicism, religion, nepotism, parochialism, sectionalism and self-centredness may be difficult to upstage and be consigned for pragmatic and holistic-based approach for improved living conditions of Nigerians under an atmosphere of trust and honesty.

INTRODUCTION

The future of any country is conditioned by a combination of factors, among which are the people, history, culture, value system, system of government, political leadership, honesty, sincerity of purpose, justice system, political ideology, economic system, and educational system.

How these factors are managed and administered within the context of equity and the people's interests and aspirations will determine the level of progression, and by extension, the future of the country. A country's future is predictable using these factors, and Nigeria presents a good case.

Nigeria is a multiethnic society with diverse cultural differences. The heterogeneous nature of the various ethnic groups makes the country eminently qualified as a sociologically complex society, particularly when viewed against the people's unflinching loyalty and primordial affinity to their respective roots and cultural values. This background shapes their thought processes, preferences, perceptions, and opinions, making the entire system take a complex form. This is the genesis and basis of tribalism or ethnicism in Nigeria.

Consequently, objectivity is overwhelmed by emotions induced by primordial attachment over issues of national importance in Nigeria. Depending on who is looking at what issues and the side of the divide on which he or she is rooted, objectivity is downplayed for parochial interest. This is evident and has almost become the norm in all strata of society, particularly in institutions and during the policy decision- making process. This also plays out at the highest level of government.

Implicitly, there is a correlation between the heterogeneous nature of the Nigerian state and its complexity. Over the years, this complexity has become a threat rather than a blessing to the corporate existence of the federation, and this is made worse by the inability of successive regimes and administrations to translate the complexity into socio-economic advantage. As a result, the country's complex configuration has continued to generate interest in the Nigerian socio-political space.

Unfortunately, the interests are not related to the outcome of any growth progression but are in relation to the discordant tunes fuelled by an inability to manage the complex nature of the country despite the country's growth potential. This experience is particularly worrisome because it poses serious concern to the future of the country. The nation is being stripped of quality policies that could engender the right framework for the peace and progress that have eluded the country over the years.

Ironically, everybody appears to be aware of this problem in the country, yet nobody is ready to openly challenge this monster by supporting measures that will promote truth, objectivity, and transparency – which apparently is the panacea the country requires to achieve peace and make progress. Moreover, the country's leadership has not been able to demonstrate enough courage to develop processes that will influence character and truth. Rather, they pretend not to know the truth, preferring to carry on as if all is well despite the ominous signs of corporate illness.

As noted, the complex corporate entity of Nigeria is a product of collective but incompatible behavioural patterns induced by powerful cultural elements. Of these elements, ethnicism and religion are the major ones that constitute a clog in the wheel of the country's progress. These elements shape and influence opinions as well as impact the decision-making process at all levels.

Consequently, the country and the various multiethnic groups that make up Nigeria struggle to live harmoniously from all fronts. But the more this is done, the more it becomes clearer that the cultural differences constitute a major challenge to national harmony and peaceful coexistence, and that has defiled the management capacity of the country's political leadership.

This, more than any other consideration, is responsible for the current reverse development in the country despite the availability of enormous resources. Whereas other countries with similar circumstances are making progress, Nigeria is not only lacking in things that engender progress but also advancing in things that encourage relapse, thereby pulling the hand of the national clock backward.

What kind of country is it where citizens, including the political class, work at cross purposes – even where it is glaringly evident that their positions are inimical to the general good of the country? I have continued to ask myself this question and have yet to receive an appropriate response. Ironically, anytime I ponder on the Nigerian entity and press for an answer, I become mystified with more questions than answers, with no hope of a probable and imminent solution. Specifically, what keeps manifesting is insincerity as a major challenge.

This is particularly frustrating because I have thought that with the older generation gradually quitting the stage, the younger generation will evolve with a neutral and unbiased mindset devoid of ethnic colouration, in order to promote and encourage national integration and patriotism. This has not happened, because the younger generations have also imbibed and assimilated those retrogressive habits fuelled by cultural differences that have put the country in its present situation, characterized by a lack of clear direction and stunted growth.

Even the National Youth Service Corps, a mandatory one-year

programme designed and introduced by the federal government to engender national integration amongst the peoples of Nigeria, has not been able to achieve its objective. Paradoxically, rather than foster unity, the programme has become an albatross, creating awareness of the deep animosity and incompatible cultural differences existing in the country. This is manifested during interaction at the various geographical areas of deployment and assignment where Youth Corpers (as participants of the scheme are fondly called) have first-hand experience of the hushed segregation going on in the country. With the exposition of the Youth Corpers to this distrustful process, which has become a Frankenstein monster, the country risks a bleak future. The future of any country is dependent mostly on the youths. If the youths are concerned by heterogeneous cultural hegemony, then there is a problem.

This is particularly worrisome when attempts by the Obasanjo and Jonathan administrations to reengineer the process of enthroning a restructured federation, aimed at addressing the salient issues threatening the unity of the country, failed to fly due to sabotage induced by entrenched interests that currently benefit the status quo. These interests are indeed the veiled power brokers with strong influence on the country's political leadership, and they activate their unholy network of conspiracies to frustrate every attempt to restructure the country by men who seek to resolve the country's socio-political bottlenecks for the good of all.

As things currently stand in Nigeria, the federation is not working, making it difficult for the country to attain its full potential. This is manifestly evident from development in the country since 1960, approximately sixty years ago, when the country attained independence from the British. The country has grown at a lethargic speed.

What, then, is the future of the Nigeria if we as a people do not have hope for the continued existence of the country as one indivisible entity? Unless we urgently act courageously to come together and discuss in frank terms the basis of our political union and how we will live together, we may as well prepare for the eventual separation.

This is the stark reality that stares at us. When people say the unity of Nigeria is not negotiable, for me, it is a statement of arrogance because it makes mockery of history. Go find out what led to countries that have broken into smaller, independent states, and why.

How do we get out of this challenge, and what are the options before us as a nation? The way out has been painstakingly provided in this book, with historical background of how we started as a nation and the contending issues that have metamorphosed to become the national question that has defied all solutions.

Time is not on our side, and the earlier we all resolve to move forward with a common purpose as a nation, the better for us. Otherwise, we risk disintegration someday, either through peaceful or forceful means.

CHAPTER 1

THE HISTORICAL DEVELOPMENT OF NIGERIA

The Making of Nigeria

Present-day Nigeria is made up of the Northern and Southern Protectorates. These were the two distinct geographical areas with separate cultural peculiarities before the advent of British colonial rule. The cultural preponderance in the Northern Protectorate is the Hausa/Fulani ethnic extraction. Other smaller ethnic groups in this area spread across the Middle Belt region, and these constitute the minorities.

In the Southern Protectorate, the Yoruba and Igbo ethnic groups in the western and eastern parts of the southern divide, respectively, constitute the major ethnic groups. Similarly, other smaller ethnic groups in this part are found in the Niger Delta region, and they make up the minorities.

In general terms, these smaller ethnic groups in both the Northern and the Southern Protectorates are called the minorities because of their small numerical strength. In either of the protectorates, these minority ethnic groups are up to approximately 120 each in numbers.

Prior to the advent of the British colonial masters, these territories had their system of administration. Perhaps for economic reasons more than any other consideration, the British authorities, under the leadership of Sir Lord Frederick Lugard, elected to amalgamate the two protectorates in 1914, resulting in the territory known today as Nigeria.

The motive for the amalgamation was not clear, but it can be deduced that it was not unconnected with achieving cost efficiency without necessarily passing the incidence of the cost of administration to the home country, Britain, apparently to reduce burden on taxpayers. This was so because the Northern Protectorate was already experiencing a budget deficit at the time while the Southern Protectorate had a robust budget with surpluses.[1]

Therefore with the merger, the British colonial masters under Lord Lugard maintained a healthy financial administrative profile, even though it was at the expense of the South, which had to be compelled to subsidize the economy and people of the North.

This singular decision of 1914 laid the foundation and set the tone for the present-day political discontent and acrimony in Nigeria. This animosity is clearly the product of the distinct cultural differences between the North and South, compounded by unhealthy rivalry induced by competitive cultural superiority.

Perhaps if the British government had done a cultural check to determine whether the people could live together peacefully and harmoniously – and by extension, check the workability of the federation – the present comatose and dubious unity that has deprived the country from experiencing progress commensurate with its resources would have been avoided. Put differently, if Lord Lugard had taken pains to determine the compatibility of the peoples from the various ethnic groups, perhaps a better alternative political arrangement would have been adopted to fit the Nigerian situation than the present federation that is not working.

Obviously, in the absence of deliberate mischief, the British colonial masters failed both in intelligence and capacity to know that the country called Nigeria was not going to work due to the heterogeneous nature of the people. Implicitly, the Nigerian people have been foisted on one another even when there are incontrovertible facts that they are incompatible and are not able to live together peacefully.

As a result, after almost sixty years of companionship, the country remained divided along ethnic lines fuelled by primitive cultural background. Therefore, rather than pay allegiance to the centre (Nigeria) through unflinching commitment, the people's loyal is brazenly displayed in favour of ethnic affinity. Unfortunately, this is why elements of patriotism, which drive development as displayed by citizens of great countries like the United States and the United Kingdom, are absent amongst us as a people.

Constitutional Development

The emergence of Nigeria as a country began with the development of various constitutions designed to provide systems of government and patterns of administration. The scope and structure of the systems of governments were indeed the reflection of the philosophy, ideology, and personalities of those who were involved in the process.

Amongst the constitutions that have so far been fashioned for the country, none contain the antidote required to assuage the fears of the minorities or other linguistic groups perceived to be marginalised. The documents lacked the trust to dissuade the urge for further agitation for amendment. This was obviously due to the complex nature of the country, with so many ethnic groupings competing for favourable deals.

Beginning in 1922, when it could be said that the process for constitutional amendment began in Nigeria (the 1914 constitution was designed to give birth to Nigeria as deemed by the colonial authorities under the British monarch), the intrigues by various ethnic interests to outwit one another for prominence have continued to hurt the polity. This was evident in the manner and approach of the gladiators involved in the constitutional creation and amendment process.

The 1922 constitution, referred to as Sir Clifford's Constitution, was the precursor of all the constitutions designed for the Nigerian entity, but unfortunately its scope and intention were meant to serve Lagos and the Southern parts. There were no representatives from the Northern parts on the legislative council. Perhaps the political exclusion of the North at the time was to allow for enough time to conclude discussion with the Emirs, who ruled over much of the territory of the Northern Protectorate.[2]

By 1946, the Arthur Richards Constitution got off the ground with the inclusion of the Northern Protectorate. Though it was an improvement of Clifford's Constitution, it set the pace for ethnic politics in Nigeria. Admittedly, it was the first policy attempt to define a constitutional and political framework for Nigeria with the creation of three regional blocks – namely, the Northern, Eastern, and Western regions – but in concept and practice, it marked the beginning of high-wire political manoeuvres characterized by political tension along regional lines. This tension had its root in the behavioural disposition of the founding fathers who, though overtly patriotic, were covertly tribalistic along linguistic leanings. Pressure and agitation, reinforced by ominous disenchantment with the constitutions by groups in the various regions, led to the need for further political reforms and amendment.

Consequently, the Macpherson Constitution of 1951 was introduced after extensive consultation with the various regional leaders, whose national vision was impaired by their respective cultural dispositions. This was evident in the philosophy behind the formation of the various political parties that were to serve as platforms for election into parliament. The National Council of Nigeria and the Cameroons (later changed to National Council of Nigerian Citizens,

NCNC) initially had a national outlook, and it had a formidable presence in the East. The Action Group (AG) was in the West, and the Northern Peoples' Congress (NPC) was in the North.[3]

Again, the operation of the 1951 Constitution further activated regional allegiance, thereby widening the dichotomy amongst the regions, particularly between the North and the South. This approach led to recurring pressure for constitutional amendments to accommodate divergent opinions as a way of dousing growing ethnic tension in the country. It resulted in the intervention of Mr. Oliver Lyttleton, the British secretary of state for the colonies, by way of introduction of a new constitution, the Lyttleton Constitution of 1954, which addressed some of the gaps in the 1951 Constitution. The gaps filled were part of the input from the country's founding fathers (leaders of various political parties), who wanted more powers and autonomy for their regions in line with federalism. This led to a devolution of more powers from the centre to the regions.

While these issues were going on, apprehension gripped the minorities within the regions that were dominated by the major ethnic groups. To reassure them of protection, the British colony then set up the Willink Commission to look into and allay their fears.

In effect, the Lyttleton Constitution was part of the design by the founding fathers to enthrone a federal system of government aimed at achieving autonomy for the regions and, by extension, fiscal federalism. Indeed, this constitution, with all the trappings of federalism, was to pave the way for the 1960 Independence Constitution with more robust features of federalism suitable for a complex, sovereign, independent state like Nigeria.

Though the 1960 Constitution was premised on a parliamentary system with features of federalism, the need to replace the Queen of England as head of state and the Privy Council as the highest judicial body, amongst others, led to the 1963 Republican Constitution with full features of federalism.[4] In the 1963 Constitution, there was a president as opposed to a head of state, and the Privy Council was replaced by a federal supreme court as the final appellate judicial authority.

Under the 1963 Constitution, besides the federal parliament, which had legislative powers under the Exclusive List, each region had its legislative council, with the Concurrent List as part of their legislative spheres. Each region also had its own constitution (to the extent that it did not clash with the federal constitution), its own police, and control over its resources up to 50 per cent (with the remaining 50 per cent paid to the centre for the maintenance of armed forces, immigration, etc.). The implication of this was that each region was able to develop at its own pace.

This was the practice until the coup of 1966, which fundamentally altered the existing arrangement. Though new constitutions were introduced in 1979 and 1999, their substances were at odds with the 1963 Constitution and thereby lacked intention and content as federal constitutions.

Fears of the Founding Fathers

The Bible says that out of the abundance of the heart, the mouth speaks, meaning that the spoken word is a product of the thought process based on a specific issue. Our founding fathers – who in this context are the leaders of the major political parties that were involved at one stage or another in the constitutional conferences leading to the making of the various constitutions – had deep reservations about the manner in which the British colonial masters bound the various ethnic nationalities together.

This raised fears, provoking an atmosphere of scepticism about the Nigerian project. Every move and utterance made by the founding fathers to one another were viewed with suspicion, particularly between the Northern leaders and their Southern counterparts. This became manifest in 1953 during the independence motion by Chief

Anthony Enahoro of the Action Group (AG) that Nigeria should attain self-government in 1956.

For the North, independence should be attained as soon as practicable, and not necessarily and specifically in 1956. This did not go down well with the leaders of the two dominant political parties in the South, leading to a motion to adjourn sine die. In reaction, the Sardauna of Sokoto, Sir Ahmadu Bello, who was also the leader of the Northern Peoples' Congress (NPC), expressed his mind. "The mistake of 1914 has come to light and I should like to go no further."[5]

What did he mean by the "mistake of 1914"? Obviously, it was the amalgamation of the Northern and Southern Protectorates in 1914, which formally coupled the two entities into one country. Sir Ahmadu Bello made no pretence about his lack of conviction for the union, and as was characteristic of him, he was never afraid to let people know for what he stood.

The NPC leader's view on the Nigerian state was also held by his deputy, Sir Abubakar Tafawa Balewa, as revealed during his address at the legislative council in 1948. He said, "Since 1914 the British Government has been trying to make Nigeria into one country, but the Nigerian people themselves are historically different in their backgrounds, in their religious beliefs and customs and do not show themselves any sign of willingness to unite. Nigerian unity is only a British intention for the country."[6]

Indeed, it was a great regret for the North that they found themselves in a union which they believed held little prospects for them, and which did not have respect for their views and vision. They preferred instead to go their separate ways, as revealed during the motion for independence. This was evident from the eight- point programme the North announced in reaction to the tension that accompanied the development over independence disagreement, which as James S. Coleman said, "if implemented, would have meant virtual secession of the Northern Region from Nigeria."[7]

In intent, content, and structure, the eight-point agenda was obviously a call for confederation. The North wanted a system of government that could protect its interests in a complex, heterogeneous political setting like Nigeria. The "eight-point programme" of the Northern Peoples' Congress (NPC), as endorsed by a joint meeting of the Northern House of Assembly and the Northern House of Chiefs, was as follows.

1. This Region shall have complete legislative and executive autonomy with respect to all matters except the following: defence, external affairs, customs, and West African research institutions.

2. That there shall be no central legislative body and no central executive or policy-making body for the whole of Nigeria.

3. There shall be a central agency for all Regions which will be responsible for the matters mentioned in paragraph 1 and other matters delegated to it by a Region.

4. The central agency shall be at a neutral place, preferably Lagos.

5. The composition and responsibility of the central agency shall be defined by the Order-in-Council establishing the constitutional arrangement. The agency shall be a non-political body.

6. The services of the railway, air services, posts and telegraphs, electricity, and coal mining shall be organised on an inter-Regional basis and shall be administered by public corporations. These corporations shall be independent bodies covered by the statute under which they are created. The Board of the coal corporation shall be composed of experts with a minority representation of the Regional Governments.

7. All revenue shall be levied and collected by the Regional Governments except customs revenue at the port of

discharge by the central agency and paid to its treasury. The administration of the customs shall be so organised as to assure that goods consigned to the Region are separately cleared and charged to duty.

8. Each Region shall have a separate public service.[8]

If you think the founding fathers from the North were the only ones who were sceptical about the Nigerian project, you are wrong. Other political gladiators, including Chief Obafemi Awolowo, the leader of Action Group (AG), expressed reservations concerning the continued corporate existence of Nigeria.

In an apparent veiled reference to the complex Nigeria project, which lacked the requisites of nationhood, Chief Obafemi Awolowo said, "Nigeria is not a nation. It is a mere geographical expression. There are no 'Nigerians' in the same sense as there are 'English', 'Welsh', or 'French'. The word 'Nigeria' is a mere distinctive appellation to distinguish those who live within the boundaries of Nigeria and those who do not."[9]

Chief Awolowo also said, "It is incontestable that the British not only made Nigeria, but also hand it to us whole on their surrender of power. But the Nigeria, which they handed over to us, had in it the forces of its own disintegration. It is up to contemporary Nigerian leaders to neutralize these forces, preserve the Nigerian inheritance, and make all our people free, forward- looking and prosperous."[10]

The fears of the founding fathers bordered mainly on the premise upon which the British founded the country. The colonial masters failed to take into consideration the ethnic and cultural differences which ultimately shape people's perception and decisions. These factors, which infuse our beings, are principally responsible for the political disagreement and distrust amongst the founding fathers.

With an attitude of frustration provoked by an inability to work on the same political page, hope for a united Nigeria gave way for despair, with concomitant panic for the possible break-up of the country. Indeed, this general negative feeling amongst the founding fathers came from parochial interests induced by tribalism and religion, which posed serious threats to the unity of the country. The country could not forge ahead with a common purpose because the allegiance of the founding fathers was more to their respective regions than to the centre as represented by the federal government. As a result, there was upsurge of frenzy fuelled by ethnic politics in almost every part of the country.

This experience might have prompted the leader of the NCNC, Dr Nnamdi Azikiwe, to prophetically assert that the country risked a bleak future due to insincerity driven by ethnicism and nepotism. Zik, as he was fondly called, had tried to project a national personality figure devoid of ethnic bias for his region, the Eastern Region. This was drowned by his fears of a possible disunited and disintegrated Nigeria. Zik had warned about this at a rally of his party, the NCNC, saying, "It is better for us and many admirers abroad that we should disintegrate in peace and not in pieces. Should the politicians fail to heed the warning, then I will venture the prediction that the experience of the Democratic Republic of Congo will be a child's play if it ever comes to our turn to play such a tragic role."[11]

I have opted to restrict this part to the founding fathers and leaders of the major political parties because of their considerable infⅼuence and persuasive capacity on their respective regions at the time. Though there are also leaders from the era after the founding fathers, who may be found amongst the military and political elites and who had also expressed their scepticism for the Nigerian project, specific reference to their statements may not find space in this work because they are outside the purview of our focus.

Today, the thought process of the various peoples in Nigeria are mainly the products and outcome of the thinking of these notable leaders. Most people in their respective regions not only believe strongly in their ideology and philosophy, but they also embrace their values and preferences. The import here is that the foundation of a house is a reflection of the concept of the owner, and the extent of investment is determined by the value he or she places on the project. Unfortunately for Nigeria, the belief of the founding fathers, which has been imbibed by their followers, is affecting the growth of the country.

The leaders in the past saw the Nigeria project as a temporary scheme with a definitive lifespan. Unfortunately, this has been imbibed by contemporary leaders. The vast majority of Nigerians do not, in their heart of hearts, believe in this country, except where the status quo favours their respective regions; that is when they reluctantly say the unity of Nigeria is not negotiable.

CHAPTER 2

THE FEDERAL SYSTEM AS AN ACCEPTABLE SOCIAL CONTRACT

Federal System of Government in the First Republic

The clarification of certain terms is imperative because of their frequent usage in this chapter. *Regions* here connote the same as units and states, and shall therefore be interchangeably used for this work. Similarly, *centre* means federal, and they shall therefore be used as substitutes for each other.

All federal systems of governments the world over vary slightly in structure and operation based on their peculiar history and needs. However, for a system to be seen as operating federalism, certain features must be present, chiefly amongst which is autonomy of the federating regions. Neither the centre nor the regions or states are inferior to one another, but are interdependent and autonomous.

Autonomy is one key feature of federalism which provides the free will by the federating regions, states, or units to act independently on issues pertaining to coordination, collaboration, dispute, bargaining, and dependence with the centre or amongst themselves, to the extent of constitutional guarantee. In this context, therefore, Nigeria could be said to have practised federalism in the first republic from 1960–1966. This is because all key features of federalism were prevalent at the time.

The federal system of government that Nigeria operated in the first republic fitted perfectly into the country's diverse cultural and ethnic composition, taking cognizance of our sociological complexities. There was a considerable level of autonomy amongst the regions, with both the regions and centre deriving their powers from the constitution. The powers, duties, and responsibilities were clearly spelt out under the exclusive, concurrent, and residual lists in the constitution. This is the essence of federalism, where there is a clear sphere of constitutional scope of operations for each of the federating units and the centre.

Were it not for the coup of 1966, when the military struck and altered that system of government, Nigeria would have transformed and grown into an enviable polity amongst its peers on the African continent and in the world. The federal constitutional arrangement at the time tacitly encouraged each region to develop at its own capacity.

One important feature of the Nigerian federation under the first republic was that the composition of the federating regions was based almost on linguistic groupings. This provided a huge advantage due to assemblage of people with identical and similar behavioural patterns, attitudes, social values, and political beliefs, making it easier for them to live together under the same inclusive government compared to other circumstances.[12] The federating units also had their own constitution, regional police, and coat of arms. Their independent style of administration had a touch of peculiar needs incidental to their culture, values, and heritage. Besides, they also enjoyed a considerable level of fiscal autonomy as guaranteed by the federal constitution, allowing the regions and the centre independent sources of revenue, including jurisdiction over a wide range of revenue wholly collected and retained by each of the two governments.[13]

Fiscal Federalism

Like any organization that requires money to function and carry out its business responsibilities, units or states in a federal system of government require money and resources to meet their statutory obligations, particularly in matters pertaining to the welfare of the people, which is the essence of government. This underscores the role of fiscal federalism and why it is of primary concern in a federation, providing the framework within which the centre (federal) and the rest of the states relate to one another. In other words, the financial relationship between the centre and states on the one hand, and amongst the states or regions, on the other, constitute the major planks of fiscal federalism.

In fiscal federalism lies a vivid description of the sources of revenue accruing to a country, as well as how this is distributed amongst the federal and states governments in such a way that no part or region is left disillusioned as a result of perceived disparity. Implicitly, there must be equity, justice, and fair play that must be not only perceived but also evidently seen to be operative.

In general terms, each region is at liberty to generate its own resources and discharge its statutory responsibilities within the limit of its resources, while also maintaining its status as an autonomous state within the federation in line with the federal constitution. This was the system that was applicable in Nigeria during the first republic from 1960 to 1966, before it was scuttled by some military officers who staged a coup to overthrow the government. Though the fiscal federalism during this period was not a perfect process, it nonetheless provided a fair basis for the economic and financial relationship that existed amongst the various levels of governments. There was no observable agitation engendered by economic injustice.

This atmosphere provided the enabling environment for the various regions to grow and develop at their individual paces.

The sources and basis of distribution of revenue were acceptable to both governments – namely, the centre and the regions. There were categories of revenue collected and retained by the federal government, and there were those collected by the federal government but credited to the regional governments according to derivation or consumption. There was also revenue collected by the federal government but allocated to a distributable pool account and shared out between the regions in the percentages of 42 to the North, 30 to the East, 20 to the West, and 8 to the Midwest. There was revenue collected and retained by the regions.[14]

Of particular interest was the revenue distributed to the regions on the basis of derivation, which was 50 per cent of the proceeds generated from rents and royalties of the mineral resources. Regions where these resources were deposited or found were paid and enjoyed this 50 per cent.

During the first republic, groundnuts, cocoa, and palm oil were found in commercial quantities in the Northern, Western, and Eastern regions, respectively. These products were the foreign exchange earners for the federal government and also major sources of revenues for these regions, from where they enjoyed 50 per cent of the proceeds. The remaining 50 per cent was retained by the centre.

The major ethnic groups in Nigeria deployed the derivation of proceeds for the development of their regions through their various regional boards, set up for the administration of these God-given resources deposited in their territories, and from which they enjoyed 50 per cent of the proceeds.

There was nothing wrong with this process until providence raised oil and gas resources in the Niger Delta, which were inhabited by minority ethnic groups. Instead of continuing with the 50 per cent derivation principle, suddenly this arrangement was altered to the detriment of the Niger Delta region. In other words, the derivation percentage accruing to the host regions of natural resources was reduced to 0 per cent.

However, after persistent pressure from the region, the government, under the leadership of Alhaji Shehu Shagari, increased the derivation to 1.5 per cent. This was further raised to 3 per cent by the Ibrahim Babangida regime until it was further brought to the current 13 per cent, as enshrined under the 1999 Constitution, which also made a provision for a further increase as appropriate. Further demand for reversion to 50 per cent derivation was frustrated by the powers that were refused.

Unfortunately, a precedent had been set regarding the percentage format for the derivation principle in Nigeria. Lack of sincerity and courage to adhere to what the major ethnic groups had hitherto enjoyed was mainly part of the problem with Nigeria. There seemed to be an obvious conspiracy of silence on the part of the major ethnic groups to deprive the Niger Delta people from enjoying 50 per cent derivation proceeds from oil and gas resources that were deposited in their God- given land. By their numbers, the major ethnic groups not only controlled the machinery of government but also had considerable and substantial inf luence in policy matters.

Principles of derivation thrive on equity, but not anymore in Nigeria. It is driven more by regional interests than equity and national consideration. This is mainly responsible for the introduction of strange and extraneous factors to determine how revenue should be distributed. What, then, is the basis of principles of derivation in a fiscal federalism?

Principles of Derivation

Derivation principle is an integral part of fiscal federalism pertaining to the allocation of natural resources on a percentage basis amongst various levels of government in a country. It is deliberately calculated to favour the geographical area or part (regions, states, or units) where such resources are found.

It is this principle that informed the basis of allocation of resources in the first republic in Nigeria. Each of the regions had natural resources from which an accruing percentage was paid, and the balance was retained in the federation account at the centre, where the federal government pooled the resources to fund the army, immigration, foreign affairs, and more. The fundamental reason behind this principle is aimed at compensating the area or region where the natural resource is discovered. Apparently, the compensation is to make up for likely environmental degradation arising from exploration and production of the resource.

The principle of derivation in the first republic also provided a sense of self-worth, economic independence, and prominence amongst the federating regions. This was because apart from their contribution to the sustainability of the centre, they had influence and control over the resources. For example, the Northern region controlled the groundnuts, hides, and skins found in that part of the country. This was also the case with the Eastern region, where coal and palm oil were available in commercial quantities. Similarly, the Western region had direct influence over its agricultural produce, namely cocoa, from which the region enjoyed derivation proceeds.

As noted earlier, during the period of the first republic, the percentage basis of distribution was 50 per cent. The federal (centre) paid 50 per cent of the proceeds for these products to the regions. In other words, each region enjoyed 50 per cent of the revenue generated from their respective agricultural produce, and the remaining 50 per cent was retained in the federal distributable account.

This system enabled the regions to enjoy robust financial health. It also engendered healthy competition amongst them because the regions were challenged to further expand their creative capacities in search of more natural resources within their geographical areas. Additional discovery was bound to translate to more revenue.

Indeed, it was a form of incentive, and this accounted for the variation in development strides amongst the regions.

While application of the 50 per cent derivable principles lasted in favour of the Northern, Western, and Eastern regions, there was no complaint or protest of any kind relating to financial and economic marginalization. For the regions, 50 per cent derivation was fair. This was the practice until the derivation principle was abrogated through various decrees.

This came at the time that oil and gas were being found in commercial quantities in the present-day Niger Delta region, which was made up of various minority ethnic nationalities. Through these decrees that were promulgated by the powers that were, the minority ethnic groups that occupied the Niger Delta region were tacitly disallowed from getting the 50 per cent derivation principle hitherto enjoyed by the other parts of the country.

The legal instrument deployed to legitimise this inequitable exercise was the Petroleum Decree of 1969 which was to later form part of the 1979 and 1999 constitutions.

CHAPTER 3

THE UNITARY SYSTEM AS THE ORIGIN OF NIGERIA'S ENDLESS DILEMMA

Transition from Federal System to Unitary System by the Military

On January 15, 1966, some young military officers led by Major Kaduna Nzeogwu violently overthrew the government headed by Alhaji Tafawa Balewa in the first republic. At the time, true federalism was in practice in Nigeria, where each region was allowed by the constitution to uphold its peculiar political identities. Though the coup was unsuccessful, it left behind a trail of blood with the death of the Prime Minister, Alhaji Tafawa Balewa; the premier of the Northern Region and Saudana of Sokoto, Alhaji Ahmadu Bello; the premier of the Western Region, Chief Samuel Akintola; and the Minister of Finance, Chief Festus Okotie-Eboh, amongst other prominent personalities.

Most of the military officers who took part in the coup were of Igbo extraction, fuelling suspicion of an Igbo agenda particularly when no significant fatality was recorded in the Eastern part of the country, coupled with the fact that another Igbo officer, Major General Johnson Aguiyi-Ironsi, emerged as the new head of state.

Rather than maintain status quo on assumption of power, Aguiyi-Ironsi abrogated and altered the federal system that was in place. He replaced it with a unitary system of government and executed this process through Decree Number 34 of 1966, which he promulgated to give legal cover to the new system. With a unitary system, all powers and authority of governments at the regional levels were ceded and concentrated at the centre (federal), making the regions serve as appendages of the centre with little or no substantial powers of their own. For Ironsi, this was the best way to effectively manage the polity even though it was antithetical to common sense and logic. By this action, he unwittingly removed the autonomy and independence of the regions, and he upset the polity, thereby laying the foundation for political instability in Nigeria.

The unitary system provoked fresh suspicion amongst the non-Igbo ethnic groups, who believed that the new system might have been a project designed to favour, strengthen, and position the Igbos above other ethnic groups. The non-Igbos' fears were reinforced by the fact that at this time, the Igbos dominated the economy and bureaucracy in the country, yet, Aguiyi-Ironsi never initiated any policy to allay the fears of other ethnic groups. This led to serious political tension in the country, culminating in the pogrom in the Northern part of the country, where Igbos were the victims. The development was apparently in reaction to loss of the autonomy hitherto enjoyed by the regions and the pattern of death in the Nzeogwu coup believed by the Northerners to have been deliberately orchestrated to eliminate its political leaders.

The resentment in the North grew and spread, leading to a counter-coup staged by some army officers of Northern origin, obviously in retaliation against the Igbos. Head of State Aguiyi-Ironsi, Western Regional Governor Lt Col Adekunle Fajuyi, and some Igbo officers were killed, resulting in the formation of a new government headed by Lt Col Yakubu Gowon.

The counter-coup deepened the animosity already created by

the Nzeogwu coup, resulting in sectional and ethnic consciousness amongst officers and men of the Nigerian army. Individual officers gave expression to this consciousness in varied peculiar ways. This was how the cohesion that had existed in the army was destroyed.

Two main reasons instigated the counter-coup. One is the perceived lopsided killings of Northern political elites in Major Kaduna Nzeogwu's coup. The second is the introduction of a unitary system of government by General Aguiyi-Ironsi, which was also perceived to be a ploy to perpetuate Igbo hegemony in the country.

Paradoxically, rather than revert to the status quo by restoring the federal system, Lt Col Yakubu Gowon retained the unitary system of government introduced by Aguiyi-Ironsi, thereby sustaining and encouraging the distrust that had robbed the nation of peace and desirable progress. In other words, Yakubu Gowon perpetuated the same anomaly that was partly responsible for the counter-coup.

The danger with the unitary system introduced by Aguiyi- Ironsi was its vulnerability to manipulation. Power and authority are centralized and concentrated at the centre, and so whosoever is head of state could deploy the apparatus of government in favour of his ethnic people, friends, and well-wishers, or he could operate parochially at the expense of national interest. This was why Aguiyi-Ironsi was not trusted with a unitary system.

The unitary system is viewed as a "winner takes all" system. This might have inspired Yakubu Gowon to sustain the system because it would obviously put so much inf luence and control of governmental powers in the hands of Northerners.

Today, the effect of this system creates ethnic consciousness, and the federal character principle introduced to allay the fears and ensure a balance is implemented more in violation of its original intention and purpose.

Abrogation of the Principles of Derivation

As noted earlier, the spirit behind the principle of derivation as an element of fiscal federalism is to ensure equity by way of compensation to the area from where mineral resources are extracted. When cocoa, groundnut, and palm oil were sources of revenue in the country, the principle of derivation was applied. That was why areas like the Western, Northern, and Eastern regions benefited from the 50 per cent derivation. The areas were inhabited by the three major ethnic groups.

However, the derivation principle was abrogated when petroleum resources were discovered in the Niger Delta, a geographical area occupied by minority ethnic groups in Nigeria. This revocation deprived the people of the Niger Delta from enjoying the 50 per cent derivation. This singular decision, more than any other consideration, is responsible for the crisis in the region today.

Naturally, this development provoked indignation amongst the people of the region, who felt cheated in a country that was supposed to protect their rights. They were unable to rationalize the motive behind the abrogation of the principles when it was now their turn to enjoy 50 per cent derivation.

Though no justifiable reasons were adduced by the government for the complete removal of the derivation principle, it could be inferred that the federal government did it to generate money for the purposes of prosecuting the Nigerian civil war, which was raging at the time. The war was between the Nigerian government and the rest of the Eastern region, which opted to secede from the country. The region was then renamed the Republic of Biafra, which subsisted until the end of the civil war in 1970, when it reverted to Nigeria.

The suspicion of the people of the Niger Delta about the real intention for the abrogation became manifest when extraneous factors like population were introduced as determinant elements of revenue allocation; these came after the introduction of the Petroleum

Decree of 1969 (later Petroleum Act 1990), which placed ownership of petroleum resources in the federal government.

As minorities, the Niger Delta people did not have a population sufficient enough to attract robust revenue. Revenue allocation was benchmarked against population. With population as a major criterion for revenue allocation, there began a general feeling of being short-changed, leading to agitation for the restoration of the principle of derivation.

The government, headed by Alhaji Shuhu Shagari, yielded to the pressure on the restoration of the derivation principle in 1980 and introduced a rate at 1.5 per cent, compared to the original 50 per cent. This was later raised to 3 per cent by the Ibrahim Babangida administration in 1992. The derivation principle was further increased to 13 per cent by the Sani Abacha administration after it was recommended by the National Constitutional Conference, set up by his administration to midwife a new constitution for the country that resulted in the 1999 Constitution.

The agitation did not end with the 13 per cent derivation as recommendation by the 1999 Constitution. The constitution had provided that the 13 per cent should be the minimum, meaning it was subject to further increases as appropriate. This open-ended provision is what has given impetus to the Niger Delta people to press for a further increase to 50 per cent, as obtained during the first republic.

Resource Control

In the absence of any prejudices, there is no conceptual muddle concerning resource control and what it represents in Nigeria. The phrase is essentially associated with the agitation in the Niger Delta for control of its oil and minerals. It is a struggle aimed at compelling the federal government to revert to the 1963 political arrangement to enable the oil host communities to be compensated for the pollution and degradation of their environment resulting from oil exploration and production activities by oil companies.

The 1963 Constitution had provided for 50 per cent derivation for the host regions where groundnuts, cocoa, and palm oil were produced. This was exclusive of the 30 per cent in the distributable pool account, which was also shared amongst the regions, including the host regions after the federal government had taken its share of 20 per cent. This is the status the Niger Delta region wants the government to revert to, because it constitutes a precedent.

Perhaps if a precedent had not been set where regions had control of their resources up to 50 per cent in the first republic, there would have been no moral basis for the agitation in the Niger Delta. The people of the region consider it both politically and economically expedient for the current 13 per cent derivation to be raised to 50 per cent, in order to enable them to control and enjoy the resources which God, in his infinite wisdom, deposited in their land.

As minorities who had little influence in the power equation in the country, the Niger Deltans are vulnerable to oppression and are apprehensive of what the future holds for the region. For them, if the rest of the country can oppose further increases of derivation for no logical reason, how could they be trusted by the time the oil dries up in the region? Will the rest of the country agree to remediate the environment that has been polluted due to long years of exploration and production activities?

They are not too sure about how the federal government will respond to their plight after the cessation of oil activities, and so they believe that the best option is to take their destiny into their own hands by a rebirth of resource control consciousness.

The former governors of Delta and Bayelsa State, chiefs James Ibori and Late Daprieye Alamieyesiegha, respectively, were arguably some of the foremost leaders from the region who risked their political careers to embark on a renewed agitation for resource control.

For the two leaders, redress of years of neglect and injustice in the area where resources are generated was imperative.

The ecosystem and aquatic life of the people whose main occupation is fishing have been negatively impacted by oil exploration activities. Their plight has attracted global attention, yet what they see more is military presence deployed by the government to protect oil facilities rather than massive development of the area.

The unitary system being practised by the country, where all powers are concentrated at the centre, is unhelpful to the plight of the Niger Delta region. A factual federal system of government and f iscal federalism like in the United States and Canada could engender an atmosphere of peace in the region.

CHAPTER 4

THE CHALLENGE OF PETROLEUM RESOURCES

Oil as a Source of Revenue for the Government

The Nigerian economy is hinged largely on oil, accounting for more than 90 per cent of total export and foreign exchange earnings, and constituting about 80 per cent of total revenue of the federal government. With an average daily production of two million barrels, oil remains Nigeria's major foreign exchange earner. Apart from being the major element of the substructure which carries the rest of the economy, it plays a crucial role in the funding of the nation's national budget. It is no small wonder that Nigeria is a monocommodity economy, reinforced by its dominance of the country's revenue stream and economic strategy.

All previous governments practically depended on oil; so too does the current government for its programmes. It is the main source of the country's foreign reserve, contributing also to the country's gross domestic product (GDP). A significant chunk of the country's budgetary revenue is generated from oil proceeds, a development that also underscores its importance in the country's fiscal landscape.

Implicitly, oil occupies a place of prominence in the revenue matrix in Nigeria. Proceeds from this important product are used to fund vital governmental programmes. Infrastructural projects being built across the country, both at the state and federal levels, are funded mainly with oil proceeds.

Its global relevance is underlined by the huge inf low of direct foreign investments into the oil and gas sector, and by extension, the Nigerian economy, which are given expression by the international oil companies (IOCs). Similarly, the Nigerian Content Policy of the government as contained in the Nigerian Oil and Gas Industry Content Development Act (NOGICD) has also encouraged the emergence of indigenous oil companies, adding value to the oil business chain in the country.

Besides the IOCs and indigenous companies involved in oil exploration and production business, there are several other foreign and indigenous companies that have heavily invested in the petroleum sector in Nigeria, creating thousands of jobs and economically empowering the people through value addition. These opportunities are available in almost all the sedimentary basins in the country.

Of the seven sedimentary basins in Nigeria – namely, Anambra, Benin, Bida, Bornu, Sokoto, Niger Delta, and Benue Trough – the Niger Delta Basin is the most productive and prolific, holding huge reserves and accounting for more than 95 per cent of exploration and production activities in the country, with huge hydrocarbon deposits in onshore and offshore (shallow, deepwater, and ultra-deepwater) acreages.

Paradoxically, the Niger Delta region from which this essential resource is extracted, and which plays host to the various oil companies, is not accorded the required attention commensurate to its contribution to the economy. Perhaps if the process of oil extraction did not impact on the environment and health of the host communities, the call for environmental remediation and compensation for the people over the hazardous effect of exploration would have been needless.

Oil as Burden on the Niger Delta

Unfortunately, the exploration and production of this all-important product has its attendant negative effects on the environment. Besides degradation of the environment and the ecosystem, oil and gas f laring also have hazardous effects on the health of the people of the communities that play host to the oil companies.[15]

The occupations of the Niger Delta people, who are traditionally known for fishing and agriculture, have been destroyed by oil exploration and production activities. They are unable to optimally and effectively farm or fish due to oil spillage resulting mostly from pipeline failures (and in some cases vandalism). Most of the environment impacted is left without complete remediation, and so the people are unable to practice their trades as appropriate.

In practical terms, the discovery of oil in the Niger Delta has brought into the region more misery than joy. If oil was never found in that area, the green vegetation and the blue sea splendour with its aquatic creatures, which are constantly under pressure from exploration activities, would have served the economic life of the people through robust programmes in agriculture and the ecosystem.

The capacity of the people to farm and fish have been undermined, and as a result, joblessness, hunger, sickness, and frustration are common and recurring trends in the region, particularly in the riverine and coastal areas. This has led to high crime rates, mostly amongst the youths who find succour in illegal oil activities like bunkering, sabotage, pipeline vandalism, and illegal refining.

The gloomy situation in the region is exacerbated by the lack of critical social infrastructure like roads, schools, hospitals, drinkable water, electricity, and marine transportation. Even where they exist, they are below the national average. There is high level of

illiteracy and poverty, inaccessibility to safe drinking water, f lood-
ing, water-related diseases, and lack of electricity. The livelihoods of
the people are profoundly susceptible to hydrocarbon pollution and
the destruction of cultivated land.[16]

There is a constant feeling of frustration amongst the host communities, who believe that they are deprived of the benefits of their
natural resources. They see the basic amenities enjoyed by employees
of the oil companies at the various oil rigs, platforms, and tank farms
located in their communities, yet they themselves have no access.
For example, they see constant electricity, drinkable water, and food
supplies at these oil locations within their communities, and they
wonder why these facilities cannot be extended to them.

Oil companies do not see it as part of their statutory responsibilities to provide these amenities for their host communities, as
long as they meet their tax obligations. They believe it is the role of
government to provide infrastructure for their host communities.
However, they often concede obligation, owing to pressure from the
host communities and the need to play supportive roles in line with
their corporate social responsibility policies, which incidentally put
a moral burden on the oil companies to initiate social development
programmes for the communities.

For the oil companies, they function within the existing laws
of Nigeria, just like in other countries where they operate. They try
to do their best through the various global memorandum of understanding arrangements they enter into with their host communities,
where agreements are reached for the provision of basic infrastructure. The attitude of the oil companies to their host communities is
a function of the legal framework governing their operations, and
hence their positions vary from country to country.

Although it is believed that the oil companies are not doing
enough, the burden of infrastructural reciprocation to the communities is supposed to be more on the government than the oil
companies in light of royalties, taxes, and equity share of the oil that

has been collected under the operating arrangement with government. In other words, the government is supposed to take absolute responsibility for the development of the Niger Delta area, if it is sincere. There is a heavy moral burden on it to do so, particularly when viewed against the backdrop of the contribution of the region to the economy, where the natural resources deposited in the region by God are used to develop the rest of the country.

Indeed, the Niger Delta is a grim reality of a region that has become a victim of long years of neglect by a country that has refused to develop and remediate its polluted environment, resulting in poverty and underdevelopment of the area.

Handouts as Alternative to the Derivation Principle

One striking feature of the 1963 Federal Constitution was the provision of 50 per cent derivation principle, which allows the region from whose territory or domain mineral resources were found to collect 50 per cent of the revenue generated from such resources. The arrangement was perfect and proved to be an antidote to bellyache. Unfortunately, this system was abandoned.

The percentage currently used for derivation principle is 13 per cent, in addition to the creation of intervention agencies as an alternative to 50 per cent. This obviously falls below the standard, and as a result, the people of the Niger Delta see the current provision as handouts deliberately offered to serve as palliative rather than a permanent cure for the root of the agitation in the region. The people want government to revert to 50 per cent derivation as a mark of equity and justice.

Anything other than the 50 per cent derivation, or massive development of the region, is viewed as a handout. If the government is sincere in its intention to develop the region, there will be manifest demonstration of efforts in this direction. It appears only a colossal infrastructural development of the region can be genuinely accepted as an alternative to the 50 per cent; otherwise, the people will continue to feel oppressed and marginalised due to their diminutive population.

The government can adopt the models used in developing Lagos and Abuja. Abuja is the capital of Nigeria, and it is the youngest major city in Nigeria, yet it is competing with Lagos in terms of infrastructure. This is because the government planned the development by setting aside a percentage in the national budget and then directly awarding contracts to reputable companies like Julius Berger for its infrastructural development, under the supervision of Federal Ministry of Works and Federal Capital Development Authority. What's more, the government directed all federal government ministries, departments, and agencies to relocate their office headquarters to the federal capital territory. That way, the development of the city assumed an accelerated pace. This can be replicated in the Niger Delta area.

What the government needs to do is draw out a master plan and embark on massive infrastructural development. It should issue a directive by asking all oil companies operating in the country to move their administrative and operational headquarters to their host communities. That way the local economy of the people will grow, with further spread of value additions.

For example, the Nigeria LNG Limited (NLNG) relocated its headquarters from Lagos to Bonny, Rivers State, where its operational base is located. This singular decision has led to a sudden boom in the local economy. Even revenue accruing to the Rivers State government through taxes of employees has increased. The Bonny people are happier for it, and this will no doubt further motivate the Bonny indigenes to protect the facilities of this gas company. Interestingly, there has not been any singular reported case of kidnapping of NLNG employee since the relocation. One can feel the peace in the texture of the atmosphere and the environment in Bonny.

This is a better approach than the provision of handouts as an alternative to genuine development. Agencies like the Niger Delta Development Commission (NDDC) and the Ministry of Niger Delta Affairs, and amnesty programmes as interventionist vehicles for the development of the area, are weak and incapable of achieving their objectives. They are incapable of responding and providing the needed infrastructure that can inspire hope and bring succour to the people.

Whatever budgetary allocation that is made to the Ministry of Niger Delta Affairs, more than 60 per cent of it goes for recurrent expenditure with little for capital projects. As for the NDDC, it appears there is a deliberate policy for it to fail. Apart from being used for political patronage and projects politically executed, the commission is underfunded.

The federal government and oil-producing companies are statutorily required to contribute to the funding of the commission, yet the government that is supposed to show good example to other contributors is a major culprit, having consistently failed to meet its obligation. The former president, Alhaji Musa Yar'Adua, once said the money owed the commission, which amounted to about N250 billion at the time and later increased to more than N700 billion, had expired, and as a result, the federal government would not pay.[17]

The former president obviously spoke the mind of the government, which is obviously a proof of the government's lack of commitment to the development of the area.

CHAPTER 5

SOLID MINERALS RESOURCES OPTIMISM

Prospects For Revenue Autonomy

Exploration of solid minerals in the country pre-dated Nigeria's independence when the colonial government started the mineral surveys of Northern and Southern Nigeria, the main features of the country's economic geology. Through the surveys, large mineral deposits were discovered in different parts of the country. These were coal, tin, bitumen, kaolin, gold, limestone and iron ore.

Among the solid minerals being processed for export today are tin (cassiterite), columbite, tantalite, lead/zinc, coal, iron, gemstone and granite, uranium and tar-sand. Those being mined for domestic use include kaolin, gypsum, talc feldspar, marble, baryte, granite and do-lomite, while minerals which are yet to be mined include molybdenum, wolframite, rutile/ ilmenite, zircon, monazite, diatomite, clays and salts

Solid minerals available in the country can be broken into five different groups, as follows:

1. Metallic minerals: Iron ore. Cassiterite or tin ore, colombite, tantalite, lead/zinc and uranium.

2. Industrial minerals: Limestone, marble, kaolin, gypsum, feldspar, diatomite, phosphate, barytes, graphite, absestors, mica, clay, bentonite, silica and quartz sand.
3. Gemstone: Emerald, ruby and garnet.
4. Precious metals: Gold, silver and platinum.
5. Carbonaceous minerals: Coal and tar sands

No.	Mineral	States where deposit are found	Estimated Reserves Metric tonnes
1.	Barytes	Plateau	5 million
2.	Kaolin	Kwara, Kastina	3 billion
3.	Bentonite	Borno, Adamawa	700 million
4.	Gold	Osun, Zamfara	2 million
5.	Limestone	Enugu	800 million
6.	dolomite	FCT, Kogi, Edo, Oyo	20 million
7.	Talc	Osun, Kogi, Niger	40 million
8.	Colombite	Jos Area (plateau)	500,000
9.	Tantalite	Jos Area (plateau)	20,000
10.	Diatomite	Borno	10 Million
11.	Gypsum	Borno, Sokoto, Adamawa	50 million
12.	Iron ore	Kogi, Anambra	110 Million
13.	Marble	Kogi	45 Million
14.	Limestone	Kogi, Benue, Ogun, Anambra, Edo, Cross River States	1.4 Billion
15.	Bitumen	Ondo, Ogun and Edo State	42 billion
16.	Lead/Zinc	Enugu, Abia, Benue, Plateau, Bauchi, Taraba, Niger and Kano States	10 Million
17.	Coal	Enugu, Kogi	3 billion

Coal and tar-sand (bitumen) have particularly attracted government's attention mainly due to the global patronage they enjoy. Nigerian coal is ranked among the best in the world due to its low sulphur and low ash content. This has the potential of attracting foreign investment, especially under a liberalised business environment. In order, therefore to optimise the opportunities in the coal industry, the Federal Government has begun moves to revive Enugu coal mines.

Government has also approved the privatisation of closed quarry sites of the Nigerian Mining Corporation, which have now been offered for sale to interested investors.

For tar-sand (bitumen), Nigeria currently has a reserve of 42 billion tonnes of bitumen. Its development would result in the production of heavy oil for refineries, as well as asphalt for the production of bitumen.

Still A Big Potential

The solid mineral sector remains largely untapped till date despite its strategic importance in the provision of raw materials and power generation, yet the sector has been neglected due to revenue derived from oil.

Besides, the overbearing influence of government and the monopoly of state-owned enterprises over this sector, contributed in no small way in impairing private sector initiatives in the solid mineral industry. But, hopes have brightened now that the government has initiated measures aimed at liberalising the solid mineral sector with a view to increasing private sector participation.

New government initiatives include review of the 1990 minerals law to make it attractive like what obtains in Zambia, Ghana, Brazil, Canada and South Africa, whose mineral laws have been well developed. There are also tax holidays of 3-5 years, deferred royalty payment depending on the size of investment, as well as strategic nature of the project.

Other incentives contained in the policy include special income tax provisions for mining companies, possible capitalisation of expenditure on surveys and prospecting operations. Investors are also required to employ the services of technically competent person while applying for a certificate of entry into the mining industry.

Developing Solid Minerals Market For Nigeria

As at today, there are no formal commodity markets for solid minerals in Nigeria unlike what obtains in Europe, United States and South African markets. This is also responsible for the sale of mineral commodities in crude form, attracting low returns and contributing to the low volume of activities and wealth creation in this sector.

This is in sharp contrast to South Africa which accounts for over 60 percent of all the mineral wealth produced in Africa, as well as Angola which is the fourth largest diamond producer in the world.

The Nigerian government aims to put the country on the solid minerals map. Government's recent policies, coupled with the growth potential of the sector have begun to attract financiers and investors to the country.

Currently, Jos, the Plateau State capital, is the hub of mining activities in Nigeria because of its strategic location, attracting most of the traders. It is expected that the proposed Nigerian Metals Exchange (NIMEX) by the private sector will enhance the fortunes of the industry.

The NIMEX is expected to provide producers and buyers of solid minerals with an organised market characterised by specification, standard and pricing system. It would also act as spring board to the world mineral commodities market.

There is a growing awareness of the inherent dangers in the

mono- commodity structure of Nigeria's economy which depends largely on the oil sector. Government's concern with diversifying is leading to focus on solid minerals development with the private sector as the engine of growth.[18]

If the solid mineral sector is well developed, every part of the country, including the states and the six geographical areas will not be apprehensive over introduction of a genuine federal system of government which allows a larger control of resources by the component states or units. This will also discourage illegal mining activities like in Zamfara and Osun states where gold is being illegally mined with proceeds going into private pockets. It is obvious from the analysis that every component part of Nigeria has the potential of harnessing its resources and optimising same for the benefits of its people.

This way, each region will develop and grow at its own pace, deploying its resources to address peculiar needs at the best ways they deem fit as against the current unitary system where the components regions financially depend on the federal government for survival.

CHAPTER 6

THE RISE OF AGITATION

The National Question, Injustice, and Insincerity

Nigeria is draped with unresolved national issues that are capable of relapsing into an albatross around the country's neck. These issues are also the forces that are pulling apart the people of the country. Every ethnic group in Nigeria today has one grievance or the other against the Nigerian state. Apparently, these resentments are products of the f lawed process that led to the emergence of Nigeria as a country.

There are about 250 ethnic groups in Nigeria that are encapsulated into six geopolitical zones: North- Central, North-West, North-East, South-South, South-East, and South- West. The groupings were based on geographical, cultural, and linguistic factors.

The South-West zone comprised Lagos, Ogun, Oyo, Osun, Ondo, and Ekiti states. The South-East zone is made up of Anambra, Enugu, Ebonyi, Imo, and Abia states. The South- South zone covers Edo, Delta, Rivers, Bayelsa, Cross-River, and Akwa-Ibom states. The North-East geopolitical zone has Taraba, Adamawa, Borno, Yobe, Bauchi, and Gombe states. The North-West encompasses Sokoto, Zamfara, Kebbi, Kaduna, Katsina, Kano, and Jigawa states. The

North- Central includes Kwara, Kogi, Plateau, Nassarawa, Benue, and Niger states.

Without exception, echoes of frustration permeate almost all strata of each geopolitical zone. It is a feeling engendered by apprehension, injustice, and insincerity, with no seriousness of purpose by successive governments to address these fears. For example, the Middle Belt in the North-Central zone is not comfortable with the introduction of Sharia law, and this raises fears amongst the people due to possible backlash. The people in the North-East, particularly those from Borno State, are not happy with the Nigerian federation over perceived years of political and socioeconomic neglect believed to be responsible for the present high poverty and illiteracy level in the area. The Boko Haram menace is arguably a manifest monster evidencing the conditions in the zone.

The ethnic minorities in the North-West, mainly of the Christian faith, are expressing fears of dominion by the Hausa- Fulani majority, who in turn are afraid of economic and bureaucratic domination by the Southern part of the country comprising of the South-West, South-East, and South-South zones.

Similarly, the South-West is complaining of the dysfunctional federation along with their South-East counterparts, leading to calls for restructuring the country based on true federalism. In a similar vein, the South-South is demanding the introduction of fiscal federalism aimed at taking control of its resources believed to have been expropriated by the federal government.

The seeming reluctance of government to address these challenges is exacerbating concomitant frustration in the country, and this is slowly but gradually killing the spirit of patriotism with a regrettable decline in commitment towards national unity – an important element required for meaningful general progress. This has thrown up so much distrust and frustration amongst the populace that people are now encouraged to take solace in promoting ethnic and religious nationalism with the hope that their interests will be better served than relying on a system that is obviously not prepared to address the contending national issues threatening integration.

The consequence of this development is the encouragement and promotion of unhealthy competition and rivalry amongst ethnic groups, particularly the major ethnic groups in their quest for national inf luence, control of political power, and national wealth.

The unhealthy rivalry amongst the various regional blocks, and by extension the ethnic nationalities, have led to the formation of ethnic bodies primarily for the purpose of protecting their primordial, ethnic, or regional interests. Ethnic bodies like Afenifere (South-West), Ohanaeze Ndigbo (South- East), Arewa Consultative Forum (North-West and North- East), Middle Belt Forum (North-Central), and South- South People's Assembly (South-South) are the result. Though their formation has sociocultural intentions, they were fundamentally created as reactions to the perceived injustices in the country. Specifically, they were designed to give voice and protection to their respective people in the different geopolitical areas.

This has led to ethnic and regional consciousness, with every section of the country scheming to have their sons at the helms of affairs, believing this is the most guaranteed way of benef iting from the distribution of national wealth. The constitution concentrates so much power on the presidency that the office holder has immense inf luence over the distribution of the nation's wealth.

This is also the reason why the office holders are reluctant to relinquish powers voluntarily, because of the value opportunities extended to their ethnic nationalities. That naturally provokes envy from other political zones, which feel cheated by being excluded from enjoying equitable political power and wealth distribution.

The situation is further compounded by the fact that the personality of the president of Nigeria is dominated by his ethnic aura, which in turn affects the seat of power, provoking unusual boldness amongst people of the same geographical area, particularly within the presidency. People therefore position and connect themselves with those in the same ethnic group with the president, because the group is believed to command considerable inf luence on the presidency for purposes of enjoying the national wealth. Those in this category are implicitly empowered, and those outside this circle are disadvantaged, resulting in so much frustration and dejection.

This has led to a strong feeling of neglect amongst ethnic groups, regions, or geopolitical zones that have no inf luence in government, encouraging corruption, injustice, suspicion, lack of patriotism, crime, apathy, disloyalty, discrimination, hate, oppression, and ethnic nationalism to thrive in our politics. This is also responsible for the strong agitation and call for the restructuring of the country based on devolution of powers, fiscal federalism, and resource control.

These issues, which have become a major source of concern to the future of the country, constitute the national question. Unfortunately, every government administration has deliberately failed to provide solutions to this national question, despite the danger to Nigeria as a country.

Biafra as a Symptom of Discontent

It is not the intention of the author to narrate the story of the Nigerian civil war that raged for three years from 1967–1970, but one must look into how ethnicism and hate interplayed to cause the war and amplify the distrust, rivalry, and unhealthy competition currently existing amongst the various ethnic groups and the different geopolitical sections in the country, with Biafra as a consequence.

The government of Nigeria under the first republic was headed by Prime Minister Alhaji Tafawa Balewa, a Northerner, from 1957 until 1966. He rose to power on the ticket of a political party, the Northern People's Congress (NPC), led by the Saurdana of Sokoto, Alhaji Ahmadu Bello, also a Northerner.

Despite the sociocultural and political differences, the country managed to forge ahead until a group of young military officers, who were mainly of Igbo origin and predominantly from the South-East region, attempted to seize power. Though the coup failed, top politicians and government functionaries, including the prime minister and the Saurdana of Sokoto (both Northerners), were killed.

Ironically, no top politician or government official of Igbo background was killed in the coup. Perhaps they escaped through providence. This elicited anger amongst the Northerners, who saw it as a deliberate ploy by the South-East to kill its leaders in order to take control of the government. This fear was given credence when the acting president of the Federal Republic of Nigeria, Dr Nwafor Orizu, an Igbo man from the South-East, invited the military to take over power.[19]

Coincidentally, the baton passed on to another Igbo officer, General Johnson Aguiyi-Ironsi.

Aguiyi-Ironsi was the highest ranking officer at the time, and going by order of seniority, he was next in command. However, exigency of morality, logic, common sense, and ethnic power equilibrium should have prevailed to know that his assumption of power would provoke ethnic sentiments and aggravate the already tense situation.

Ethnic and sectional interests took prominence in judgement and were freely deployed as a discerning factor in the circumstance. Is it morally right for officers from a particular region to eliminate key government officials from another section, inadvertently paving the way for persons from the same section that initiated the coup to take over control of the government? For the Northerners, it was injustice and a plot by the South-East section to seize political power; it could not be rationalised under any guise. Indeed, the whole development was perceived by the Northerners to be a script that was deliberately rehearsed.

National interests gave way for primordial sectional interests. There was a violent reaction by the Northern region through reprisal

attacks on the Igbos and their interests. In what looked like a re-
venge mission aimed at overturning the political tide, some young
military officers from the Northern section of the country launched
a counter-coup, killing the head of state, General Aguiyi-Ironsi.[20]
Yakubu Gowon, then a lieutenant colonel from the North, emerged
as the new head of state and commander-in-chief of the armed
forces.

This led to general disenchantment amongst the Igbos, who believed they were being persecuted unjustly with the reprisal attacks.
For them, the silence by other ethnic groups and sections amounted
to conspiracy against the people of the Igbo nation, and they began
to develop a sense of betrayal, rejection, and hate.

After a series of failed attempts to resolve the issues, includ-
ing the meeting and agreements reached at Aburi, Kampala, and
Addis Ababa, the then military governor of Eastern Nigeria, Lt
Col Odumegwu-Ojukwu, with the approval of the Consultative
Assembly, reacted by proclaiming the Eastern Region an indepen-
dent and sovereign state, the Republic of Biafra.[21]

The decision did not go down well with the federal government,
prompting the head of the Nigerian government, Lt Col Yakubu
Gowon, to endorse full military action against the secessionists. A
civil war ensued and lasted for three years.

Despite the "no victor, no vanquish" position of the federal government, Biafra has become an article of faith amongst the Igbos.
They believe Biafra is a struggle against imperialism, neocolonialism,
and slavery. To them, it's a fight for freedom, self-determination, and
independence.[22] Ironically, the younger generation, who were not
even born at the time of the civil war, have been caught in the web
of the Biafra spirit. Perhaps the story passed on to them has become
a propelling force that has continued to encourage them to push for
the actualisation of the country of their dreams.

The independent state of the Republic of Biafra still exists in the
minds of the average Igbo man, and perhaps this is the reason why

the struggle has been sustained to this date, fifty years after the end of the Nigerian civil war. The support base of this struggle within and outside the country is a clear indication of the premium placed on Biafra by the Igbos.

The entry into the Biafra project by youths forecloses any hope that the struggle for the actualisation of Biafra will end soon, and this is the real danger as demonstrated by the series of protests organised by the youths and their determination, even in the face of confrontation with security agencies. Today, besides the Movement for the Actualisation of the Sovereign State of Biafra (MASSOB), there is a splinter group named the Indigenous People of Biafra (IPOB), making the struggle a complex risk for the Nigerian state.

Nevertheless, the agitation for Biafra is no doubt a symptom of discontent and larger dislocations in the Nigerian federation as currently constituted.

Militancy as Sign of Frustration in the Niger Delta

The pressure that led to the setting up of the Willink Commission in 1957 by the British colonial administration was the precursor to the current agitation that has degenerated into militancy in the Niger Delta. The commission was set up to allay the fears of the minorities over their future in a country dominated by the three major ethnic groups that had influence and control of instruments of government. It was a system where the majority had its way, and it put the minority in an inferior and dependency position in perpetuity.

As it turned out, the fears expressed by the minority over likely oppression by the majority were made manifest when oil was discovered in the Niger Delta, a minority region. The majority, which controlled the machinery of government, not only used their power to readjust the derivation formula to their advantage, but they also ensured, through the Petroleum Decree of 1969, that the derivation principle was abrogated, leaving the Niger Delta with nothing.

Hitherto, the derivation principle was 50 per cent when natural resources were found in the territories of the majority ethnic groups.

Besides that, the majority ethnic groups have consistently used their numbers to outwit the minority group in the Niger Delta, aimed at depriving them from achieving their demand for control of the hydrocarbon resources in their land that hold much promise with huge commercial value in foreign currency. Even where the Niger Delta people ask for compensation due to the pollution suffered from the effect of oil exploration, it is the majority who defines and determines what the nature, form, and compensation for the hazardous effect on the health of the people and the environment should be.

Demands and suggestions from the Niger Delta people that are at odds with the position of the majority are usually viewed as unpatriotic, selfish, retrogressive, and subversive. Perhaps because of their influence and control of governmental powers, they do not see anything wrong using resources from the Niger Delta to develop the rest of the country without adequately compensating them, despite the subsisting precedent where 50 per cent derivation was applied to natural resources found in the territories occupied by the major ethnic groups.

The disposition of the major ethnic groups toward the Niger Delta region came to the foreground during the 2005 National Political Reform Conference (NPRC), convened by former President Olusegun Obasanjo. Delegates from the Niger Delta region had demanded for 25 per cent derivation of natural resources with a yearly increase of 5 per cent until it reached 50 per cent. This request was opposed by delegates from the geopolitical zones dominated by major ethnic groups.

As a result, the Niger Delta delegates staged a walkout when they could not persuade other delegates to accept their request. Entreaties for an understanding in view of what the region contributes to the economy were rebuffed by other delegates, mainly from the major ethnic groups. It appeared the absence of the Niger Delta delegates provided a convenient field to arrive at far- reaching decisions because there were no concerted efforts to reach out to the Niger Delta delegates to return to the f loor of the conference.

What's more, the politics surrounding the non-passage of the Petroleum Industry Bill (PIB) could also be traced to the Niger Delta region. In the bill, the issue of 10 per cent fund for host communities has consistently been opposed by the National Assembly members who are from mainly the major ethnic groups. Although the authors of the original PIB saw the need to compensate the host communities with the 10 per cent as a way of motivating them to protect oil facilities, legislators from the major ethnic group in the National Assembly saw it as unnecessary.

They contended that the Niger Delta region was already enjoying 13 per cent derivation, and so it did not deserve an additional 10 per cent. It is on the strength of this really that the passage of the PIB has been stalled, despite its importance and capacity for the growth of the oil and gas industry, and by extension the country's oil proceeds.

Notwithstanding the opposition to matters that will improve the conditions of the regions, the elders and other notable stakeholders have also tried to lobby and reach out to inf luential people in other regions to prevail on the government to address the plight of the region, with no success. This has further worsened the hopelessness prevalent in the region, particularly amongst the youths.

The youths from the region believe their resources are being carted away by the country without remorse or plans for compensation. For them, there is a need for justice and equity, and because there is no evidence of government's commitment to developing the region, they have resorted to draw the attention of global community to their plight through militancy and kidnapping of expatriates and local oil workers alike. These activities were carried out under the aegis of the Movement for the Emancipation of the Niger

Delta (MEND) and the Niger Delta Avengers (NDA). Though other smaller bodies also sprung up, masquerading themselves as freedom fighters for the cause of the Niger Delta, their relevance could not be situated within the context of the Niger Delta struggle.

The amnesty programme initiated by former President Umaru Musa-Yar'Adua to dissuade the youths from resorting to arms struggle has not yielded any meaningful result despite the fact that several youths who gave up their arms benefited from the scheme through training and skills acquisition. Its inability to address the fundamental cause of the Niger Delta challenge is the reason why the arms struggle has yet to abate.

Put differently, the frustration and deprivation in the region resulting from years of neglect without any hope of redress, despite the contribution of the region to the economy, prompted the youths to take up struggle, calling for the practice of true federal system of government and fiscal federalism to enable them take control of their resources. The arms struggle in the Niger Delta is clearly a case of discontent in the Nigerian state.

CHAPTER 7

RESCUE EFFORTS

Failed Attempts at Resolution

In the absence of any charade, it is crystal clear to everyone in the Nigerian political space that the current Nigerian federation is not working and incapable of delivering on the collective aspirations of Nigerians as a people. As a result, successive governments in the country had tried without success to resolve the dysfunctional federation through policies and actions considered appropriate to make up for the gap and enable it to work. Yet the more these measures are introduced, the more the inadequacies and injustices of the system are exposed. Perhaps this is due to the application of wrong tools in addressing the situation, which invariably throws up the wrong result.

The current system, which in all practical purposes is a unitary system, has proved to be inefficient. It is indeed part of the Nigerian problem, and unfortunately the country's leaders do not see it from this perspective. They failed to accept the fact that restructuring the country into a true federal system is what is required to resolve the national question at this time; otherwise, it is like applying malaria medication for the treatment of a cancerous tumour.

The application of a wrong solution induced by insincerity and hypocrisy has contributed in no small measure to def lating the country's growth capacity. Rather than muster political courage and deal with the issue of true federalism once and for all, our leaders hide behind a smokescreen of patriotism to introduce cosmetic measures unsuitable and incapable enough to balance the federation and restore confidence in the polity. These measures are deployed to buy time through false engagement, leaving the people with a phoney sense of hope for equity and justice. Some of these measures include state creation, federal character principle, and National Youth Service Corps (NYSC) scheme. Attempts have also been made using various national conferences as vehicles to drive a restructuring process, and all to no avail due to extraneous factors relating to selfishness, ethnicism, and loathing.

Take state creation, for example. It was a method deployed by the federal government to balkanise the country into several states, giving a false impression of a rejig of the federation into a true federal system of government. The country, which initially had a four- regional structure in the first republic, currently has a total of thirty-six states created by past administrations. No doubt, state creation has further weakened the hitherto regions, and the states have become the appendages of the government. Rather than resolve the contending issues, the problems still subsist.

Indeed, the states not only are perpetually at the mercy of the federal government but also depend on the centre for survival. The administration of states in the country has reconfirmed and exposed the profundity of a unitary system of government and, by extension, subservient corporatism in the country. The states have become so weak to the extent that they cannot survive without funding from the federal government, making them incapable of resolving the national question.

The federal character principle is one tool the government has also deployed as elements of federalism. It was introduced to ensure a balance and equity in matters relating to appointments at all levels, including the Federal Executive Council, ministries, departments, and boards of agencies and parastatals. This has also failed to address the national question. Besides encouraging and sacrif icing merit on the altar of representative bureaucracy or federal character principle, compliance is sacrif iced on the altar of tribalism and favouritism. People who are not qualified are appointed to sensitive and critical positions in the country without regards to the negative impact on the economy and future of the country. Indeed, it is now a "Who do you know?" connection to get appointed.

The National Youth Service Corps (NYSC) was created to engender unity in the country through cross- regional posting of young university and polytechnic graduates to enable them to deploy their skills and knowledge for the development of their motherland. During this task, they are expected to become acquainted with the culture and people in their primary areas of assignment. The NYSC scheme has also not achieved its objective because corps members or participants are now more disillusioned and elicited by waned patriotism engendered by system contradictions.

Also, attempts by past presidents of the country to resolve some of the contending national issues through national conferences have also failed to achieve the desired purpose. Of these conferences, the National Political Reform Conference (NPRC), constituted by former President Olusegun Obasanjo in 2005 and former President Goodluck Jonathan in 2013, were distinct due to obvious, genuine intention to strengthen the country's unity and democracy through restructuring of the polity. However, these were frustrated by contentious issues induced by narrow and conf licting sectional interests.

It must be noted that the clamour for the restructuring of the country into a true federal system of government is championed mainly by people from the southern parts of the country, which is made up of the South-West, South-East, and South-South geopolitical zones. It is therefore not a coincidence that the two former presidents who pursued the restructuring of the country with sincerity of purpose and vigour through the national conferences were both from the southern parts of the country.

Those from the North-West, North-East, and North- Central geopolitical zones have not hidden their reservations for the restructuring of the country, preferring instead the status quo. Given their overwhelming numbers, inf luence, and control in government with all the trappings of a unitary system, there is a natural proclivity to resist true federalism, obviously owing to economic and political advantage. This is why the North and the South maintain different stances on issues pertaining to restructuring and true federalism in the country.

The situation is made more complex as most delegates to these conferences went there with preconceived mindsets dominated by sectional interests rather than national interests. In some cases during debates, tempers and emotions run high, leading to tension that further put the country at risk of division on ethnic and regional lines rather than enduring unity.

When genuine efforts are initiated and aimed at providing a solution to the country's daunting problems, there are those who believe that such a move may jeopardise their narrow interests and put their regions in a disadvantaged position. With this position, all manner of political gymnastics is displayed to inf luence decisions of proceedings in their favour. These are some of the fundamental reasons why the conference reports could not be implemented to reshape and restructure the country into true federalism, as originally intended.

Impact on Nationhood

A country whose constitution and system of government are not founded on the free will of the people is bound to provoke suspicion and alienation. Not only may it disconnect from the aspirations of the people and make them vulnerable to manipulation, but the country risks a cloud of uncertainty over its future. In such a country, citizens may be reluctant to discharge their obligations, and disloyalty, dishonesty, lack of patriotism, and recalcitrance may become common features.

Take patriotism, for example. A country cannot demand patriotism from its people; it is earned and never forced. It is driven by sheer belief in a country's constitution and values. When a people have absolute confidence in a system of government, they demonstrate unequivocal zeal to support the ideals the country represents. They become exceptionally and passionately disposed and committed to give their best, particularly in matters relating to nation building, without reservations. That is why there is a correlation between patriotism and national growth. Countries whose citizens are not committed to their country's systems and values do not make as much progress as those with nationalistic citizens.

In Nigeria, patriotism is uncommon, and it is because the country's system of government does not inspire the kind of confidence required to spur people to action. If the progress of any nation depends on the people, yet their loyalty to the constitution and other value systems that will help the country attain nationhood is in doubt, then there is a capital deficit. This is the problem with Nigeria, and it can be situated in the dysfunctional federal system with all the trappings of a unitary system. Perhaps this also explains why, unlike Europe, the United States of America, and other developed countries, the Nigerian national flag is hardly hoisted or put on display by individuals and organisations. The few places where it is on display are not driven by patriotism but by mere routine exercise and corporate aesthetics.

Another example is corruption. This is a silent national killer that sprouts out of greed engendered by scarce resources and disbelief for a country. Corruption, which is a big industry today in Nigeria, is a product of the current dysfunctional federalism. There is general scepticism as to whether the current system has the capacity to guarantee the security of lives and property, as well as support the aspirations of citizens. Besides, most Nigerians doubt the continued existence of the country because of the inherent injustice in the so- called federal system. As a result, people seize any available opportunity to commit fraud and partake in unwholesome practices to generate unearned income to support their future.

This is why corruption has defied all government attempts to nip it in the bud. Indeed, it has become a way of life because most top functionaries at the highest and lowest levels of government, including civil and public servants, are caught up in the corruption web. Even the private sector, which hitherto enjoyed some considerable level of immunity, has become a victim.

Corruption stinks everywhere in Nigeria, and it is a lack of true federalism that encourages it to thrive. There is hardly an office you enter, whether in the public or private sector, where corruption will not leave its signature on the transaction. Corruption has taken a toll on the country, slowing down its progress and killing aspirations and dreams engendered by diminished patriotism. That is why the current war against corruption initiated by President Muhammadu Buhari may not succeed until the country is restructured based on true federalism.

The absence of true federalism is also promoting ethnicism in the country. Decisions are driven by ethnicism and sectional interest rather than by national consideration. People are more concerned with what will benefit their people, their areas, and their geopolitical zones. This is why ethnic groups lobby for political appointments for their sons and daughters: so they could use their offices to influence projects and cause development in their areas. This also accounts for the lopsided and uneven development in the country. Ethnic groups without representation in government have no voice, and by implication they suffer infrastructural deficit. Implicitly, the desperation by ethnic groups to influence projects to their areas is informed mainly by scepticism over the country's lifespan and weak political system.

Lack of true federalism also accounts for why the country does not have accurate census figures today. Because population is one of the criteria used for allocation of resources, Nigeria has not been able to conduct an acceptable census due to manipulation, with the ensuing credibility problem. Thus, the current population, just like the previous ones, is based on estimation. How do you then plan and make progress as a nation without accurate census figures? This is one of the prices the country is paying for the dysfunctional federal system of government.

Honesty has been thrown to the wind. Even the government is no longer trusted by the people, who have also risen to outdo one another. Citizens are compelled by uncertainty to embark on a rat race with dishonesty as a vehicle for achieving quick results. No one is sure of the future. In schools, in government and non-government institutions at all levels, and in all facets of our lives, honesty has become a scarce commodity. You can hardly find a sincere person, all because the dysfunctional federalism promotes fear over the country's future.

In Nigeria today, there is so much fear and anxiety rising from unhealthy competition and rivalry amongst ethnic groups, particularly amongst the major tribes (namely Hausa-Fulani, Yoruba, and Igbo). Overwhelmed by their size advantage, they use their numbers to oppress others, particularly the minorities. For example, they put aside the off icial language, English, as lingua franca to communicate in their native language in official circles and offices. Most times this is done with arrogance and without any iota of respect to the dignity of the other person or persons who may not understand the language. Under these circumstances, those who cannot communicate in their native language are never taken into confidence in offices, and as a result, they suffer psychological def lation.

The growing communal rife amongst ethnic groups in the country is one of the consequences of this development. There is hardly any ethnic group that does not have an army of youths who have transformed into ethnic militia for the protection of their community or area – for example, Odua Peoples Congress (OPC), Amotekun, Movement for the Emancipation of Niger Delta (MEND), Bakassi Boys, Egbesu, Coalition of Northern Youth Associations (CNYA), and Niger Delta Avengers (NDA). The emergence of these bodies is fuelled by a lack of confidence in the government's capacity for protection. This is one of the dangers the country faces as a result of sustained deceit in a f lawed system of government. Killings and reprisal killings across national divides have become a recurring challenge: the Fulani herdsmen and farmers, religious- induced conf licts, the indigenes-settlers crisis, and other ethnic-based related clashes across the country.

Indeed, the impact of the dysfunctional federalism on nation-hood is legendary, profound, and a capital deficit that has provoked an unfathomable feeling of frustration and revulsion amongst the populace.

A Country on the Precipice

Current development in the country suggests the future is bleak, even as concerns surge. The concerns stem from lack of faith in the capacity of the country to faithfully discharge its obligations under the current f lawed federalism, though arguably it is responsible for the lopsided opportunities, disproportionate allocation of resources, infrastructural disequilibrium, and inappropriate administration of policies. The current tension in the country is an accumulation of fears engendered by the unresolved national question, which has given impetus to the assertion that if nothing was done to redress this injustice, the country may be sitting on a keg of gunpowder.

Interestingly, more than ever before, the call for restructuring of the country has assumed a more audacious dimension and is on the upward swing, gaining momentum with the army of those in favour of restructuring swelling by the day. It is reaffirmed that in order for the country to make progress and enjoy peaceful coexistence amongst the various ethnic groups, the government has the responsibility of managing the process and ensuring that the country is restructured in line with the wishes of the majority of people.[23]

The word *restructuring* has become a common feature in the country's political lexicon and is the subject of national discourse. Anywhere one goes, it is the subject of discussion. It is a recurring topic in offices, beer parlours, schools, marketplaces, worship centres, hospitals, prisons, theatres, bus stops, beaches, airports, motor parks, relaxation spots, and commercial buses and taxis. In all of this, the present government's apathy and continued silence to this growing concern is unhelpful and is capable of aggravating the already tense atmosphere. The people are restless and livid; they need justice and want the country restructured. To remain mute and pretend as if nothing is happening is like heating up the already charged situation. For example, the Afenifere, Ohaneze, Pan Niger Delta Forum (PANDEF), and a few vocal minorities in the North are all calling for a restructuring of the country.

The agitation by Indigenous Peoples of Biafra (IPOB) has further raised the bar on the issue of self- determination. IPOB members have taken to the streets, holding rallies and agitating for an independent country of their own, using and displaying the national f lag of Biafra as a symbol of their struggle. Its precursor, the Movement for the Sovereign State of Biafra (MASSOB), is making passionate pleas with the United Nations to conduct referendum for the South-East geopolitical zone, aimed at achieving an independent state of the Republic of Biafra.[24]

In a similar vein, another group, the Movement for the Survival of Niger Delta Indigenes (MOSUNDI), has commenced agitation for self-determination and independence from Nigeria. In a letter to the former secretary-general of United Nations, Dr Ban Ki-Moon, and signed by President Prince Samuel Amaiwo, Chimezie Ezebunwo Timothy, Hon. Okan Obukohwo Okan, and spokesman

Godgift Edigbe, MOSUNDI seeks for a United Nations–supervised referendum for self-determination of the Niger Delta Peoples of Nigeria based on the UN charter, articles, resolution, International Court of Justice decision, and the Scotland referendum.[25] In addition, the Niger Delta Self- Determination Movement (NDSD), led by Annkio Briggs, is also pushing for self-determination for the people of Niger Delta region.[26]

Also, as part of the pressure on the government to meet the aspirations of the people, the Niger Delta Avengers, a youth organisation waging an arms war against oil companies in the Niger Delta region in retaliation for government's inaction in addressing the developmental needs of the region, has asked the United Nations to free the Niger Delta people from Nigeria, threatening to declare the region a country of its own as well as display its currency, f lag, and passport. [27]

Notable Yoruba leaders have also threatened to break away from Nigeria, alleging incessant and unprovoked attacks, as well as the invasion of their farmlands by Fulani herdsmen. The leaders held an emergency summit in Ibadan, Oyo State, titled "National Insecurity and the Menace of Fulani Herdsmen in Yorubaland." The meeting, presided over by the former governor of the Western Region, General Adeyinka Adebayo, warned that the Yoruba will no longer tolerate the present structure of the country, which they claimed undermine self-actualization of the people of the South-West. The summit cited incessant cases of rape, destruction of economic plants that form the bedrock of the livelihood of locals, the armed violence unleashed by the nomads, and the consequent cultural disequilibrium that the displacement of people from crisis-ridden Northern Nigeria has brought to communities in Yorubaland. Factional leaders of the Oodua People's Congress (OPC), Dr Fredrick Faseun and Otunba Gani Adams, were unanimous in saying that the time to "leave Nigeria" and assert the sovereignty of the Yoruba people is now.[28]

Also, leader of the Yoruba World Congress (YWC) and renowned historian, Professor Banji Akintoye, warned that the break-up of Nigeria is imminent if the leaders failed to restructure the country properly to address concerns of all nations that make up the country. This was contained in the Sunday Tribune of May 10, 2020 which reported there were "concerns over the risk of Nigeria breaking up with some ethnic nationalities pulling out of the union which appeared to have been heightened with the admission of the Yoruba and Igbo nations into the Unrepresented Nations and Peoples Organisation (UNPO)."

In a similar development, Middle Belt Minorities under the auspices of the Association of Middle Belt Ethnic Nationalities (ASOMBEN) had also set up a ten-man committee to prepare a draft position paper on the restructuring of Nigeria. In a communiqué issued at the end of ASOMBEN's one-day meeting in Jos, Plateau State, to brainstorm on the likely position of the Middle Belt on the restructuring, the summit resolved to gather opinions from stakeholders and put together a Middle Belt position on the subject within the next six weeks. The group had earlier shared a working document in which thirty-nine of them called for some form of the restructuring of the country but expressed disappointment that only one came from the Middle Belt.[29]

Today, hardly any Nigerian can define what the country stands for in terms of its vision. It is certainly not a country of equal opportunity. Those with connections at the top get juicy contracts and jobs for their people. Securing employment in Nigeria is no longer a function of merit and intelligence; it is based on who you know, or your direct or indirect connection with people in authority. That is why there is a growing population of unemployed youths with good academic backgrounds but without jobs and the means to live; most of them are people who do not know people at the top. No wonder, therefore, that PhD holders now apply for jobs as drivers in Nigeria.

Even people or artisans who opt for small- and medium-scale businesses are quick to close up shop due to the absence of infrastructure like electricity to support their dreams. Many become frustrated with no hope of business rebound. Most families, particularly the low-income groups, are f inding it increasingly difficult to provide food on the table, and in some cases they are unable to fund the education of their children.

The rising youth unemployment in Nigeria is now a major source of worry with the World Economic Forum (WEF) and the Lagos Business School, saying the country sits on a "time bomb". Unemployment is raising the existing risk of insecurity and militancy in major parts of the country, as well as undermining the government's efforts at fighting insurgency in the North-East, uprisings in the South-East, and other serious crimes in parts of the country.[30] The growing cases of kidnapping and other crimes are engendered by hunger and suffering. The country is indeed sitting on a time bomb.

Unfortunately, increase in inf lation, unemployment or under-employment with economic discomfort, and negative consumer sentiment have led Nigeria's misery index to be on the rise in the last two years. Nigeria's unemployment rate stands at about 13.9 per cent, underemployment is at 19.7 per cent, and the inf lation rate is 18.55 per cent, pushing Nigeria's misery index to a record 52.15 in the third quarter of 2016 – the fourth highest in sub-Saharan Africa.[31]

It is therefore imperative for the country to initiate urgent measures to address the national question so as not to further endanger the corporate existence of Nigeria.

CHAPTER 8

THE HARD SOLUTION

Options before Nigeria

Where do we go from here as a country, having allowed our sense of good judgement to be drowned on the altar of tribalism, ignorance, corruption, selfishness, parochial interest, hate, interethnic hostilities, dominion complex, ego, pride, envy, jealousy, ethno-religious rivalry, power plays, arrogance, ethnic superiority complex, greed, and self-centredness? These attributes are products of the mind, generated and processed from the heart, making Nigeria a complex and difficult puzzle.

Nigeria fought a civil war before, and the price was costly both in human and material terms. It was an attempt by South- East Nigeria to secede from Nigeria and form the botched Republic of Biafra. We have yet to recover from that war, which lasted for three years, and the scars of the conf lict are still fresh in our memories. Nigeria cannot afford a second civil war because we may not be twice lucky. The outcome of such a war cannot be predicted.

The country is nonetheless in a dilemma. Without any form of warfare, the blood of innocent people is being shed on a daily basis through premeditated attacks by Boko Haram, Fulani Herdsmen, militants, kidnappers, armed robbers, and other criminal elements.

The country is under severe pressure and stress, induced by bottled-up tension capable of exploding and bursting into f lames.

It is becoming crystal clear that the current system lacks the built-in capacity to manage and give the people a common vision. The best option is to root for the most suitable system of government that will take into consideration the multiplicity of interests as encapsulated in the various ethnic groups and cultures in the country. This can be through a re-examination of alternative systems of governments like proper federalism and confederalism. If this option fails, we can peacefully opt for a break-up of the country. These options remain the best in the light of the current unitary system redressed as federalism, which has completely failed to work, and paradoxically its deepening ethnic rivalry and animosity in the country.

If, as a country, reason is deliberately prevented from prevailing, then the remaining option is to balkanize the country, preferably through peaceful means. The option of violence as a means of disintegration will not do anybody good in the long run. The better option remains peaceful means, where the federating units can go their separate ways without firing a shot and destroying innocent lives and properties. Modality for the peaceful severance of relationships can be easily worked out.

Through this way, there will be no bloodshed, and humanity will be spared the agony of war. This may also free the resources of the world body, the United Nations, which is likely to intervene to manage the resultant effect of a humanitarian crisis in the event of war.

Therefore, in the absence of deceit and hidden agenda, the options are clear: restructure, or deconstruct to dismember. Put differently, the country's political leadership should muster the courage to face the truth by restructuring the country to operate a system of government based on true federalism. Otherwise, confederalism or break-up should be explored.

Unitarism, Federalism, Confederalism, or Break-Up

In all practical sense of the words, the unitary system is what is currently being practised in Nigeria, even though it is repackaged and branded to look like federalism. In other words, the unitary system of government has been tested and found to be unsuitable for Nigeria's peculiar circumstances.

One major feature of the unitary system is that the states depend on the centre for survival. All the states of the federation in Nigeria today depend on the federal government through allocation of funds that are disbursed on a monthly basis. As a result, the states have become weakened, an appendage of the centre with little or no creative ability for revenue generation.

Perhaps because they're tired of dependency, the states' governors devised a strategy where pressure is exerted on the centre through assertion of their relevance within the political space. A pressure vehicle known as the Governors' Forum was created. The formation was primarily designed to collectively put pressure on the federal for robust bargain procedures. So far, the aim is being achieved because the governors have succeeded in several occasions to compel the presidency to succumb to their wishes. The Governors' Forum has also strengthened their collective power of resistance from the ravaging inf luence of the centre, as a way of deepening their bargaining hold on the federal government.

It is the weakness of the unitary system to deliver on the country's peculiar needs, which has given rise to the call for true federalism. People believe in the power of true or proper federalism to resolve Nigeria's daunting challenges. It is borne out of antecedent. Having been practised during the first republic, its capacity to address the country's peculiar multiethnic complexities is no longer in doubt.

Fiscal federalism, which is an essential element of federalism, will ensure equity in the administration of revenue. The pattern of revenue distribution has always been a bone of contention between the federal (centre) and the states on one hand, and amongst the states on the other hand. Therefore, the principles of derivation serve as a mechanism against revenue injustice and oppression, because nature has bequeathed upon every state or region natural resources that can be harnessed for revenue generation.

However, where true federalism fails to be accepted as a system of government, the option of confederalism should be explored. A confederal system of government is an assemblage of smaller states or regions agreeing to form a country and ceding some key services to the central government. The member states have a greater level of autonomy. Each state under this system exercises independent jurisdiction over specific areas considered critical to its people, history, tradition, and autonomy, including legislative rights. The scope of responsibilities of the central government is confined to areas like immigration, army, foreign affairs, common currency (though the states are in some cases allowed to have their currencies), and in some cases customs.

It should be noted that under the confederal system, member states that desire to discontinue with the central union or government have the right to do so. Put differently, every member state is at liberty to pull out of the central government or country. However, in doing so, a referendum is conducted to ascertain whether the decision to pull out is borne out of the free will of the people. It is the wishes of the people, as confirmed by the result of such a referendum, that will determine the final decision whether to go or remain. The Swiss canton system, the former Soviet Union, and to a larger extent the United Kingdom are good examples of a confederal system.

The complete break-up of Nigeria may not be the right option. No matter the multiethnic rivalry fuelled by suspicion and disagreement amongst the various ethnic groups, there are also several advantages living together under a political entity.

The share size of the country is an advantage both in terms of commerce, security, and global respect. If Nigeria breaks into smaller independent nations, the respect it currently commands in the comity of nations will wane. It is therefore imperative for a deeper ref lection on this option. Rather than opt for a complete break-up, it is better to adopt either true federalism or confederation. In this way, we still maintain the country's common heritage and national identity.

However, like an unworkable marriage that is persistently enmeshed in irreconcilable crisis, where at the end either party – namely, the man or woman – parts ways either alive, deformed, or dead, it is better Nigeria opts for complete break-up, particularly if it is established beyond doubt that the country can also not survive as a nation under a true federal or confederal system of government. This can also be done peacefully. A peaceful disintegration remains the better option owing to the attendant benefits, including assets sharing. In war, assets are destroyed and human lives wasted.

Referendum as a Rescue Valve

The steady escalation of tension in the country can be doused if the ruling class can throw pride to the wind and chart the part of peace and honour in their approach to resolving the current challenges facing the country. Through a referendum, the people can decide which system of government to adopt. Referendum is a political instrument for resolving political questions. It is an aggregation of the wishes of the people over which political direction to go. In this context, a referendum can be conducted in Nigeria to decide on the system of government that best suits the country's current circumstance.

Therefore as a way out of Nigeria's political impasse, it is suggested that a referendum should be activated to resolve the country's contending political issues. Let the people decide which way they want to go – unitary system, true federalism, confederation, or break-up – because the failed unitary system is no longer an option. For how long will the country's leadership suppress the voice of the people? Giving the people a voice and using a platform like a referendum will help to heal the wounds of a decade that has defiled several cosmetic medications.

Amidst confusion over which direction to go, countries all over the world have explored the option of referendum to resolve their political differences. Indeed, it is a rescue valve deployed to pave the way forward and end indecision over issues of national importance. Referendum is about the future of the people, and it provides an opportunity for people to decide the future of their country.

If the government is about the people and their future, it would be appropriate to allow the wishes of the people to prevail. If a referendum had been deployed all these years, perhaps this lingering call for a change in the country's system of government would have fizzled out, and a new political order with clear direction would have emerged. At this stage of Nigeria's political life, a referendum provides the opportunity to rediscover the country's future through assertion of the free will of the people.

The sustained call for a change of political system is a clear indication that people are not satisfied with the current system of government. This makes the unresponsive attitude of the political leadership a grave concern and a matter of discontent, given it's failed to offer headway on the political crisis. It will be in the overall interest of the citizenry for the government to conduct a referendum. This option remains the finest opportunity for the government to demonstrate its willingness to yield to the demand of the people. Not conducting a referendum will only exacerbate the current situation and deepen the growing apprehension over the future of the country.

Therefore, for the love of the country, the younger generation, and even those yet unborn, it is a political capital for government to conduct a referendum devoid of any conditionality as part of deliberate efforts to steer the country away from the edge of the precipice. This will not only inspire confidence but also reinvigorate the trust of the people regarding the government's capacity to meet their aspirations.

Indeed, a referendum is a pathway and a rescue valve to resolving the current national question with the concomitant effect of an enduring peace process. For posterity, it is imperative for the government to take bold decisions on matters that will provoke enduring joy amongst the greatest number of citizenry for the overall good of the country.

Playing politics with the national question and putting up a nonchalant disposition amounts to deliberately downplaying the import of the issue. Deductively, it is tantamount to further pushing the country beyond the cliff where it currently stands. Indeed, inaction by successive administration constitutes a risk that stirs at every Nigerian on the face, mind, body, and soul. A referendum will surely dispel the raging danger.

CHAPTER 9

THE FUTURE OUTLOOK

A blessed nation with potentials

Nigeria is a country that cannot be ignored by comity of nations. With over 180 million people, it is a commercial hub for goods and services originating from the developing and advanced economies. This explains the essence of its trade relations among nations, and why multinational corporations, either physically or through their products, have their presence in Nigeria.

These transnational companies play key roles in the Nigerian economy either through direct investment and participation or through proxies in the power, transportation, telecommunications, agriculture, manufacturing, education, housing, health, petroleum, oil and gas sectors, among others.

As the most populous black nation on earth, it symbolizes the strength, future and hope of the black race, playing prominent role in global affairs. Its citizens strive for excellence, displaying a spirit of resilience and industry aimed at attaining prominent height in their areas of competence and endeavours. There is hardly any part of the globe a Nigerian professional may not be found contributing to the development of his host community.

In Africa, Nigeria plays a father-figure to many of its counterparts, using its influence to promote peace across the continent. This was particularly profound in the 1970s when Nigeria made Africa the centre-piece of its foreign policy. Indeed, it is the biggest economy in Africa with huge human, material and natural resources, making her the Rock of Africa.

From the pool of its human capital assets, Nigeria assist some of the African countries to build structures and institutions, particularly in education as epitomizes by the Act establishing the Nigerian Technical Aid Corps, through which Nigeria renders manpower and technical support expertise to African, Caribbean and Pacific countries aimed at fostering South-South Cooperation.

Its roles in world affairs as demonstrated in the United Nations, African Union, and other transnational platforms are profound. Among its West Africa neighbours, Nigeria is the economic destination, providing a support base for their economies. From antecedent, whenever Nigeria has cause to shut its borders, its neighbours go through excruciating socio- economic pains, thus, making sure her immediate neighbours draw from her sea of affluence.

I recalled growing up in Warri back in the good old days, you were proud to be a Nigerian. There was availability of good and functional infrastructure. Electricity was at optimum level with rare presence of blackout. The educational system was effective and efficient. Good roads, housing and drinkable water were dominant. All roads in Warri were fixed with street lights and public toilets and water. Security was not a challenge as my friends and I could go clubbing all night and return home safe to the arms of our parents.

What about those sound moral values we imbibed from our parents? The national etiquettes as encapsulated in the family values drained your desires to stay out of corruption and be contented, appreciating what you have. This was not peculiar to Warri as this experience also played out in other parts of the country. Where are the values today children can look up to?

There was no palpable segregation, nepotism, ethnicism or

tribalism. Even if there was, they were diplomatically, equitably and judiciously managed. Aspirations knew no perimeter, as any person with the right credentials and qualifications could rise to any height. Limits were never defined by your ethnic grouping. From West to the East and from North to South, there was a common purpose and vision despite the disparities in tongues. We tolerated and accommodated one another. Things are no longer what they used to be, making Nigeria a paradox of itself and a strange country with missed opportunities.

Suppressed hopes and missed opportunity

The failure of the political system and the leadership to deliver on a genuine process for unison, honesty, love, integrity, development, peace, is a missed opportunity and major threat to the country's future. The leadership failed to take advantage of the political consensus leading to the country's independence thereby missing the opportunity to build a virile nation stripped of malice.

It is apparent that the political configuration handed over to the Nigerian leadership at independence was primed to fail as it contained elements of potential crises and contradictions. Yet, the leadership could not recognize and close these tragic gaps. By their leadership style, they further encouraged and fueled the forces of disunity and distrust by allowing other elements of political discord embedded in the polity to thrive.

As a heterogenous society with subterranean ethnic nationalism, the leadership could not anticipate and rise above ethnic sentiments, bigotry, religious leanings and primordial penchants. At independence when they took over the reins of power from the British colonialists, they had no political ideology, making them vulnerable to political manipulations. When a man is not sure of where he is headed, his path will be determined by the whims of others.

This lack of political ideology was what informed the frequent change of party membership, resulting in cross- membership of parties, decamping from one political party to other. Ethnicism was, and remains the major driver of cross- membership of parties. Though financial inducement is also a consideration, ethnicism took over the void created by lack of ideology. This practice which started in the First Republic before the Nigerian civil war has become a re-curring culture in the Nigerian political space, dominating thoughts and perceptions.

A people's future depends on the intellectual capacity and integrity of leaders with clear focus and vision. However, when leaders demonstrate lack of these attributes, hopes become dim and the future exposed and predictable. Countries that have grown their countries from developing economies to advanced world, were driven by visionary leaders with clear focus. Nigeria lacks such visionary leaders.

The leadership is drenched by gab of ethnicism, failing to live above ethnic biases, and preferring to give priorities to matters of provincial interests. By their conducts, these traits are openly displayed at the expense of national priorities, and the trust reposed on the people are betrayed. Implicitly, the political leadership has allowed ethnicism to breed and spread to all facets of life, becoming an albatross in the Nigerian political space.

Therefore, the Nigeria's experience does not inspire hope and possibilities for the future which is further compounded by other threatening elements like nepotism and unpatriotic disposition, which in Nigeria, are direct offshoots of ethnicism. These have caused in no small measure in subduing and capping the dreams and aspirations of many citizens, particularly those in private business and those with ambition of rising to the pinnacle of their careers, either in the public or private sectors.

Regrettably, no visible or appreciable efforts have been demonstrated by the political leaders towards building bridges of trust and unity by way of solution. Thus, ethnicism has blossomed to become a major stumbling block to national harmony and compromise, posing serious threat to the country's future. In Nigeria today, decisions are driven by this monster and it does not matter at what level, be it federal, state, or local government level. Even the corporate and business atmospheres are not spared as they have been held captive by ethnicism.

Ethnicism is unhelpful to national unity and aspirations. Except the leaders demonstrate resolve to nip this monster in the bud, it will continue to throw up challenges like corruption and crime which have practically taken over the Nigerian society. Corruption and crime are currently in upward swing with no hope of abating. Indeed, corruption and crime are driven by the hopelessness in Nigeria.

Where there is no hope, initiatives and patriotism are impeded, resulting in release of creative energies and resources to perfect and package corruption and crime to look resourceful. Those who engage in crime and corruption do so to contain frustration and achieve self-sufficiency and protection. This is why the country's progress is not commensurate with its human and natural resources endowment.

If the country's leadership is sincere and is desirous of inspiring hope and confidence in the polity, I suggest the first thing is to tackle ethnicism. One sure way of going about it is to launch an orientation campaign with the theme, "Same Citizen, One Nation, One Vision"; and then pragmatically and sincerely drive the talk with convincing confirmations. The thrust of this campaign will be to de-emphasis ethnicism in all forms and colouration from our national psyche, which should be intensively and vigorously canvassed. This should lead to abrogation of "state of origin", "quota system", "settlers status" from the country's statutes.

The outlook ahead

Looking ahead, Nigeria's future is dependent upon the willingness of its government to cooperate and ensure enthronement of genuine processes for the benefit of the people. Prospects and promises held by the future are threatened daily due to self-serving policies designed to serve provincial rather than national interest, an experience that is further compounded by government's deliberate attempts to overlook rising challenges.

In other words, there are recurring infractions and frustrations in Nigeria due to deliberate attempts by government not to contain loathsome practices, indicative of its sympathy and support for sustainability of such heinous practices, so long as it is self-serving. Ominous evidences stare at everyone; yet, nobody is able to react except one whose bullock is jabbed. Those who benefit from corruption and nepotism are opposed to change while victims of the same system cry for justice.

Perhaps, a few examples are imperative to further demonstrate the Nigeria's experience and what the future holds. For clarity purposes, cross-institutional and sectoral references, which are by no means exhaustive, are deployed to support a clear understanding of why the future of Nigeria holds little or no optimism and prospects for people. In other words, government's lack of moral and political capital to contain societal deficits offer dim hope for the future.

The primary role of the Executive arm of government which hosts the Presidency of Nigeria is to implement the laws enacted by the Legislative arm of government. Implicitly, enormous responsibilities rest with the Executive, controlling over 60 percent of national budget to discharge its responsibilities. Yet, its conduct does not inspire hope. Court judgments are not respected and rule of law are suppressed by the Executive.

The three arms of government that are supposed to offer checks and balances on one another to ensure delivery of good governance for the benefit of the people are in unhealthy contest with one another. The Executive uses its agencies to hound down the Legislature and the Judiciary. The Legislature on the other hand, uses its powers to hold the Executive hostage in matters concerning approval process of budgets and appointments.

The Judiciary on the other hand, allows itself to be intimated by the Executive or out of self-fish interest, commercialize judgements, even though its remunerations are guaranteed under the Consolidated Funds. Implicitly, there is constitution but no constitutionalism. This problem is not just a recurring phenomenon but is growing worse by the day, thus putting a doubt on the future of the country.

Besides these unhealthy institutional rivalry, the Legislature and the Judiciary arms of government are also not immune from corruption syndrome. Apart from "budget padding", a new lexicon describing inflated expense heads or insertion of new and additional budgetary spend, the Nigerian legislators get away with "Constituency Allowance" meant to empower and support their electorates, but often times are diverted and unaccounted for. If those who make laws for the country cannot be trusted, what then is left for the future?

In the Judiciary, judges have been dismissed for cases of corruption involving procurement and pervasion of justice, casting serious doubts in the justice system of the country. As the last bastion of democracy, constitutional and social process, what hope is left in the future of the country if the common man cannot get fair judgement or are not convinced that the judicial process is balanced, fair, honest and transparent.

Mortgaging the country's future through unwanted loans is one area that is of primary concern. Both the federal and the state governments are groaning under huge debt profile due to excessive borrowing. The impact of these loans is not felt by the average Nigerian as they are drained by misapplication, misallocation, misappropriation and mismanagement under the guise of recurrent expenditure and miscellaneous issues. What is the ratio of public servants to the rest of the population? The government needs to learn from the United Nations Conference on Trade and Development (UNCTAD) on the principles governing loan procurement. Unfortunately, there is no indication of policy reversal, creating a dark cloud of sustained mortgage around the country's future.

Corruption stinks in all the ministries, departments and agencies (MDAs) of government. It is also the same at the state and local government levels where corruption flourishes like a booming enterprise. For example, it is impossible to obtain any type of genuine licence from any government agencies without paying bribe. Corruption has become a way of life to the extent that even helpless applicants seeking employment in government establishments are compelled to pay bribe before they are short-listed. So under these circumstances, what kind of future awaits the country?

The country's sporting events are stunted because the institutions responsible for sports development are weighed down by corruption. Football at the local league level is not developing because of corrupt practices where administrators, coaches and referees are key actors. Matches are fixed with impunity as those involved harbour no fear of arrest and prosecution. A club playing host to a visiting team hardly loses a match, as outcome of matches are predetermined. Perhaps, this is also responsible for why Nigerian referees are hardly graded by The Fédération Internationale de Football Association (FIFA).

The Federal Ministry of Youth and Sports Development only concentrates on sports, leaving the youths to their fate. There is no articulated programme aimed at secured future for the youths. Most of them, for lack of what to do, resort to gambling, using platforms like BET9JA, Naijabet, Baba-Ijebu, etc. What a future? Perhaps, that is why a good number of them now resort to drugs as temporary relief mechanism to enable them to forget the reality on ground. Specifically, medications like cough syrup, tramadol and codeine which offer cheaper alternative to cocaine, heroin and Indian Hemp, are used to suppress hopelessness in the land.

A foray into the country's educational sanctuary demonstrates that Education is in a state of decay in Nigeria. This is supposed to be the base of the future of any society as it serves as ladder to the top. Developed nations who know the secret of education invest so much in it. In Nigeria, nothing inspires. Education's share in the national budget is meagre within the context of its criticality in national development. Since there is not enough budget to support this sector, the people and the institutions established to drive this sector resort to self-help, either to augment budget shortfall or simply for survival.

This condition has thrown up many vices. Arbitrary fees are charged, unqualified teachers are recruited, examination papers are leaked, "Sorting" system where students settle teachers/ lecturers materially or sexually is pervasive, quota system where students with lower marks are admitted while those with higher marks are disqualified based on state of origin that is dubiously classified as "educationally advantaged states". In other words, those from "educationally disadvantaged states" have higher chances of admission, while those from the "advantaged states" are deprived of admission through imposition of higher cut-off marks, thereby lowering their chances of admission, and by extension, their progress. What a country and its future?

Even some professors who run the business of academics with the devotion of brewed educationists who are supposed to be role model devoid of primitive practices are held captive by the corruption web. By their exposure and background, professors are light bearers and path finders. In Nigeria, some of their contributions hardly go beyond teaching, relegating research and other scholarly initiatives to the background due to engagement of unrelated practices.

When I was growing up in Warri, Nigeria, there were technical colleges like Sapele Technical College and Atamakolomi Trade School where artisans were trained in various technical skills in carpentry, electrical works, plumbing, tailoring, bricklaying, etc. Today, these institutions across the country have ceased to exist, and private efforts are not robust and effective enough, resulting in poor services. Youths from neighbouring countries like Republic of Benin, Togo and Côte, d'Ivoire who are well trained in various trades in their countries now enjoy better patronage than Nigerians. Since you cannot give what you do not have, what then is the future of the Nigerian youth?

A country of about 180 million people cannot generate up to 5,000 megawatts of electricity. Yet, there is no hope of improvement. So, how then can the artisans and the small- scale enterprises survive? It is a pathetic situation given the revenue that have gone down the drain under the watch of successive governments under the guise of improving power supply. Governments efforts at improvement are weighed down by impunity and corruption, casting serious doubt on power supply prospects in the country.

Sectors like Agriculture, Aviation, Transportation, Finance, Oil & Gas, Mining, Tourism, Banking, Insurance, and others are also not spared in the whirlpool of corruption, where even the saints, unwittingly, fall victim because of potent network of collaborative pressures deliberately built around the system. For the Nigeria Police Force, its reputation for corruption is legendary, and there is insufficient space to accommodate its chronicles.

Nigeria does not know the exact number of its population as current figures are premised on guess work due to inability of the National Population Commission (NPC) to conduct accurate census. Statistics generated from census is what any serious economy uses to plan and determine areas of critical socio- economic intervention. In advanced economies, everybody cooperates to make headcount a success. In Nigeria, greed, self- centeredness and provincial interest arising from ethnicism have diminished any chances of credible and accurate population figure in Nigeria. The NPC charged with the conduct of census just exist in name. Its capacity is weakened by the heavy weight of ethnic, sectional and parochial regional interest's intrusions. People see population as means and access to larger share of the nation's revenue since it is statutorily a major determinant for revenue sharing and allocation.

The population headcounts of 1962, 1963, 1973 and 1991 were all marred by controversies resulting from falsification and manipulation of figures induced by parochial, sectional and ethnic interests. Today, population figures are based on estimation, and planning has been made difficult. When a country does not know its population, budget and planning are impaired, resulting in backward movement. Indeed, this is a glimpse of what the future holds.

Just like the NPC, it is extremely difficult for the Independent National Electoral Commission (INEC) to conduct free, fair and credible election in Nigeria. Like its predecessors, INEC's activities are heavily influenced by the ruling political party, and this is borne out of desperation to hold on to power and the nation's resources. Apart from President Goodluck Jonathan who humbly conceded defeat in the 2015 presidential election, no incumbent has been defeated. Incumbent administrations deploy government apparatus, including use of security agencies to skew electoral results to keep them in office. The underpinning motive behind this exploit is retention of power aimed at self- service, greed, narrow ethnic and sectional interests rather than national interest. So, where is the future when a system cannot freely produce competent leaders based on the wishes of the people?

The Nigerian Customs Service and the Nigerian Immigration Service are two institutions that have become metaphor for corruption. When a person is recruited into these para-military agencies, he or she is congratulated as he or she may soon experience upward swing of status due to huge inflow of unearned income resulting from corrupt-based life-changing illicit transactions. That is why it is possible for foreigners to be able to obtain the Nigerian Passport from Immigration with ease, if he or she was ready to cooperate or collaborate directly or with designated agents. Indeed, it is a cash-and-carry service. Obviously, this is the future, as it is beyond redemption.

For the Customs, this is where some importers and businessmen hold sway. Some of them have been able to penetrate the system to the extent that they enjoy undue waivers or illegally negotiated rates for their goods. At the land borders and seaports, the practice is the same. This is also responsible for why Customs officers are reluctant to proceed on annual leave because of fear of losing their unearned daily income. Government and the nation lose so much revenue through these leakages and unwholesome practices which have become a sustained norm. Since this practice cannot be curtailed, it will continue to rub off on the country's future and its prospects.

Prostitution in Nigeria used to be an abomination. Not anymore. It has no more boundaries and barriers, as survival predispositions has made it a big business. It is now openly or covertly practiced. In some places, some of the married women are not left out, giving the single ladies a competitive run. This cannot bring glory to any nation but shame. Unfortunately, this commercially induced promiscuity is conditioned by the economy, and the government is to blame for the rising trend. Refusing to yield to the demand for restructuring aimed at improved living conditions for the people with resolute determination to curb corruption, makes government an accessory. What a future?

The political leadership has consistently failed to see the entire country as one constituency desirous of attention. The leaders are drained by primordial and parochial interests. What kind of country where its president will encourage development imbalance like when President Muhammadu Buhari said those who gave him 97 percent votes will benefit more than those who gave him 5 percent votes. Ironically, the resources of the country being relied upon for development come from the Niger Delta area which gave him 5 percent votes. Even for Mathematicians, 97 and 5 percents do not add up, making it a complex scenario. What a future awaits Nigerians?

Every new day in Nigerian raises new security, economic, political and future concerns with concomitant possible depression. Nothing to look forward to. It is no small wonder people are fleeing from the country in droves. Those leaving Nigeria for other advanced economies are not limited to low-income people, but even successful businessmen and professionals in various fields of endeavours are also relocating from Nigeria. The driving force is obviously fear of the unknown aggravated by the form and void mirrors by the future.

Indeed, it is a gloomy picture since those with large population and political dominion, who invariably, controls the resources, are opposed to restructuring of the country, causing diminished hopes and frustration in the land.

The points highlighted in this chapter are just a tip of the ice-bag of what goes on in Nigeria. They represent a few of the gamut of clogs that have weighed down the country, precluding it from getting to its "Promise Land". It is unfortunate that the leaders who are obviously disconnected from the popular wishes of the people crying for equity, are not perturbed, as most of them have alternative homes abroad where they can take shelter in case the country goes out in flames.

Unless the country restructures, and allow the prevalence of a proper federal system of government in place, discontent, ethnicism, disunity and unpatriotism will continue to hold the country backward with no prospects for the future, leading to eventual de-amalgamation and balkanization of Nigeria.

CONCLUSION

Peace is one of the essential ingredients of life that man tries to achieve in his quest for livelihood. The underpinning motive behind his daily struggles is to live a life devoid of troubles, where he can create wealth and enjoy it under an atmosphere of peace. Without peace, life becomes miserable and may not be worth the brawls. Victims of wars or people whose territories have been turned into theatre of war have a better appreciation of the word *peace*.

If an issue is diagnosed as a potentially inf lammable disease in a country, it is always important to take proactive measures to nip it in the bud before it snowballs into a larger problem that may be difficult to handle. Proactive measures are more cost effective than damage-control processes. In other words, it is cost inefficient to allow a problem to persist when it can be contained. This is where the call for restructuring Nigeria can be situated. If the subsisting unitary system of government is adjudged to be characterised by injustice and partiality, then a redress of it is imperative and should take the front burner in the country's political space.

The genesis of Nigeria's trouble has its roots in the Amalgamation of 1914, where the British deliberately failed to take into consideration the cultural differences and incompatibility of the people of the Northern and Southern Protectorates, which were collapsed into a single country that became Nigeria. Since then, the country has not known real peace because all its efforts to move forward have been enmeshed by manifest and invisible inhibitions, resulting in intractable crisis. The Nigerian civil war, fought between 1967–1970, is just one of those many troubles that have befallen this country as a result of the questionable intention of the British colonial masters.

More than sixty years after attaining independence in 1960, Nigeria has failed to grow into maturity, exhibiting all known symptoms of a child. Every attempt to move forward as a country has been frustrated and drawn backward by centrifugal forces engendered by cultural heterogeneity. However, the multiethnic cultures notwithstanding, if the country was a product of a thorough pre-amalgamation negotiation, it's most likely these unending mutual suspicions amongst the various ethnic groups might have been forestalled.

People are able to work in unison when there is a common purpose, but where unity and trust are absent, people will work at cross purposes with no particular direction. It is this peculiar situation that Nigeria has found itself in and that is prompting discerning questions whether Nigerians are one. This pertinent question, which has become a recurring thought process for many, is due to the discordancy in the country's system of administration.

Perhaps this led Femi Fani-Kayode, a former minister of aviation, to ask in an article, "Is Nigeria really one nation or is she many nations forced to remain within an artif icial, unworkable, and unsustainable entity? Are our people really 'bound in freedom, peace and unity' as our national anthem proudly proclaims or is that just a deceitful mirage and never- ending illusion? Is our marriage and amalgamation borne out of consensus and a genuine desire to remain together or borne out of compulsion?"[32]

The bane of the problem is traceable to the country's leadership, which is unable to make a separation between primordial attachment and national interest. This deficit is helping fuel distrust and lack of faith in the entire system. Prior to the coup of 1966, the distrust was within a manageable limit, but it grew in intensity thereafter.

The abrogation of the federal system and the subsequent replacement with a unitary system by Major General Johnson Aguiyi-Ironsi further widened the gap in the suspicion's web.

The autonomy hitherto enjoyed by the regions or states under the federal system was completely lost to the centre under the unitary system. Implicitly, the regions were and are still controlled by the centre, and their capacity for growth and development are conditioned upon the whims and caprices of the powers that be at the federal level. This led to fury and a deep feeling of frustration and cynicism.

The loss of regional autonomy was one of the reasons for the counter-coup of July 1966 that brought General Yakubu Gowon to power. Ironically, instead of restoring the federal system, the administration continued with the unitary system despite a reversal of the power equation with the erosion of autonomy at the regions and the retention of overwhelming powers and authority at the centre. Since then, peace has eluded the country, and each region or state wants back its autonomy and a level of independence that can support its socioeconomic aspirations based on resource control rather than being conditioned by the centre.

As part of the agitation for a return to the federal system, where the regions or state could have a meaningful level of control over their affairs and resources, the Niger Delta region has been pushing for an increase in principle of derivation to the level of the pre-1966 coup. The South-West geopolitical zone is also not left out of the call for a return to a true federalism, just as the South-East region has not hidden their disposition towards confederation. These agitations are borne out of frustration.

No serious attempts have been made to address these frustrations, which are growing by the day. The few attempts at resolving the national question through various constitutional conferences are either cosmetic or sabotaged by deep-rooted interests that favour the current unworkable system of government because of the benefits they derive, despite its lopsided, favourable impact. This has further raised fears of negative backlash owing to the growing agitation in response to the government's unresponsive attitude at resolving the contending issues.

The growing agitation for the restructuring of the country portends grave danger to the peaceful coexistence of the country, and it will therefore not be in the best interest of the government to ignore this ominous development. A stitch in time saves nine, they say. Nothing should be taken for granted. The government should rise to the occasion and yield to the demand of the people. Restructuring does not mean the country should be dismembered or balkanised. It is simply a change of the system of government from the current unitary system, characterised by heavy concentration of powers at the centre with a weak substructural base at the state level.

Indeed, there is tension and growing discontent in the country, and these can be felt in the texture of the atmosphere. The situation has the potency of escalating. Rather than wait and waste available resources to contain upheavals, the government could save lives and properties by restructuring the country to run on true federalism in line with the wishes of the people. In the absence of a genuine federal system, the country can still opt for a confederal system of government. It is only when this option fails that arrangement for break-up of the country could then be worked out.

To determine these lines of actions, a referendum offers a good window for the government and the people. A referendum should be deployed to ascertain the wishes of the people regarding decisions and the veracity of choices. The government can leverage on the outcome to embark on the next steps, which would obviously have the support of the people. Through this process, a stamp of legitimacy would have been placed on the choice of the people, whether such choices are in favour of federalism, confederalism, or break-up.

A country's future and the extent to which it can deliver on its aspirations are products of the constitution and the leadership.

Unfortunately, the system of government as encapsulated in the Nigeria's constitution and the ethnic-driven personalities of its leaders clearly define the limit the country can reach. In other words, the country's future is bleak as long as the political leadership who are currently benefiting from the status-quo are averse to restructuring of the country.

There is nothing inspiring about Nigeria anymore as long as there is political domination by one ethnic group or section of the country, as the constitution and the dysfunctional system of government has made it possible for those in control of political power to control the entire resources of the nation which has left no hope for the political losers, most of whom are the minority ethnic groups.

Lack of trust for the system has amplified the misery and frustration level in the country with corruption as a common leverage to make up for the shortfall created by those who control leadership and the resources.

It is no small wonder Nigerians who have lost confidence in the system are leaving the country in droves as the future does not inspire any optimism anymore.

Indeed, Nigeria is a study in reverse political psychology, which is also useful as lessons for emerging heterogeneous democratic societies.

ENDNOTES

1   Wikipedia, the Free Encyclopaedia.
2   Billy Dudley, *An Introduction to Nigerian Government and Politics* (Macmillan Publishers, 1982), 42.
3   Richard L. Sklar, *Nigerian Political Parties* (NOK Publishers, 1963), xiii.
4   www.lawnigeria.com.
5   Richard L. Sklar, *Nigerian Political Parties*, 128.
6   Sir Abubakar Tafawa Balewa at the Legislative Council in 1948. "Quotes of Founding Fathers on Nigeria", *Vanguard Newspaper*, 1 October 2016.
7   James S. Coleman, *Nigeria: Background to Nationalism* (Berkeley: University of California Press, 1958), 300–400.
8   Richard L. Sklar, *Nigerian Political Parties*, 132; *Daily Times*, 22 May 1953.
9   Path to Nigerian Freedom (1947); http://w w w.obafemia wolowofoundation.org/awo quotations.php.
10 The Peoples' Republic (1968); http://w w w.obafemia wolowofoundation.org/awo quotations.php.
11 Dr Nnamdi Azikiwe, Premier of Eastern Region, at NCNC rally, Urualla, Nigeria, 1964.
12 E. O. Awa, *Issues in Federalism* (Benin: Ethiope Publishing Corporation), 26.
13 S. Egite Oyovbaire, *Federalism in Nigeria* (London: Macmillan Publishers Ltd), 69.
14 S. Egite Oyovbaire, *Federalism in Nigeria*, 70.
15 *The Guardian*, 24 February 2017, 8.
16 Human Rights Watch, *The Price of Oil: Corporate Responsibility and Human Rights Violations in Nigeria's Oil Producing Communities*, 95–97.
17 *Vanguard*, 20 January 2008.

18 Mike Owhoko, "Solid Mineral Resources" in *Nigeria: Politics, Economy, Business and Investment Opportunities, 2000 – 2001*, (Verity Communications Limited}, pp.123-128

19 Emeka Odumegwu-Ojukwu, *Because I Am Involved* (Spectrum Books Limited), 30.

20 Karl Maier, *This House Has Fallen: Nigeria in Crisis* (Penguin Books), 13.

21 C. Odumegwu-Ojukwu, *Biafra: Selected Speeches with Journals of Events* (New York: Harper & Row Publishers), 170–177.

22 C. Odumegwu-Ojukwu, *Biafra: Selected Speeches with Journals of Events*, 358.

23 Shola Oyeyipo and Segun James, *The Insurmountable Restructure Struggle, This Day Newspaper*, 23 January 2017.

24 *Vanguard Newspaper*, 12 September 2016.

25 *Urhobo Today*, 20 May 2015.

26 *Vanguard Newspaper*, 29 November 2015.

27 *Vanguard Newspaper*, 13 May 2016.

28 *Vanguard Newspaper*, 9 October 2015.

29 *Independent Newspaper*, 14 July 2016.

30 *The Guardian*, 26 January 2017.

31 *Business Day Newspaper*, 24 January 2017.

32 *This Day Newspaper*, 23 December 2016.

CPSIA information can be obtained
at www.ICGtesting.com
Printed in the USA
LVHW090139210620
658110LV00003B/369

9 781480 890083